Jeremy Fernando

Reflections on (T)error

D1741943

Jeremy Fernando

Reflections on (T)error

VDM Verlag Dr. Müller

Imprint

Bibliographic information by the German National Library: The German National Library lists this publication at the German National Bibliography; detailed bibliographic information is available on the Internet at http://dnb.d-nb.de.

Any brand names and product names mentioned in this book are subject to trademark, brand or patent protection and are trademarks or registered trademarks of their respective holders. The use of brand names, product names, common names, trade names, product descriptions etc. even without a particular marking in this works is in no way to be construed to mean that such names may be regarded as unrestricted in respect of trademark and brand protection legislation and could thus be used by anyone.

Cover image: www.purestockx.com

Publisher:
VDM Verlag Dr. Müller Aktiengesellschaft & Co. KG
Dudweiler Landstr. 125 a, 66123 Saarbrücken, Germany
Phone +49 681 9100-698, Fax +49 681 9100-988, Email: info@vdm-verlag.de

Produced in Germany by:
Schaltungsdienst Lange o.H.G., Zehrensdorfer Str. 11, 12277 Berlin, Germany
Books on Demand GmbH, Gutenbergring 53, 22848 Norderstedt, Germany

Impressum

Bibliografische Information der Deutschen Nationalbibliothek: Die Deutsche Nationalbibliothek verzeichnet diese Publikation in der Deutschen Nationalbibliografie; detaillierte bibliografische Daten sind im Internet über http://dnb.d-nb.de abrufbar.

Alle in diesem Buch genannten Marken und Produktnamen unterliegen warenzeichen-, marken- oder patentrechtlichem Schutz bzw. sind Warenzeichen oder eingetragene Warenzeichen der jeweiligen Inhaber. Die Wiedergabe von Marken, Produktnamen, Gebrauchsnamen, Handelsnamen, Warenbezeichnungen u.s.w. in diesem Werk berechtigt auch ohne besondere Kennzeichnung nicht zu der Annahme, dass solche Namen im Sinne der Warenzeichen- und Markenschutzgesetzgebung als frei zu betrachten wären und daher von jedermann benutzt werden dürften.

Coverbild: www.purestockx.com

Verlag: VDM Verlag Dr. Müller Aktiengesellschaft & Co. KG
Dudweiler Landstr. 125 a, D- 66123 Saarbrücken,
Telefon +49 681 9100-698, Telefax +49 681 9100-988, Email: info@vdm-verlag.de

Herstellung in Deutschland:
Schaltungsdienst Lange o.H.G., Zehrensdorfer Str. 11, D-12277 Berlin
Books on Demand GmbH, Gutenbergring 53, D-22848 Norderstedt

ISBN: 978-3-8364-3781-3

Dear Mr Cook,

One never begins to even think without the help of one's teachers. I would like to thank you for all the years of learning and most of all your friendship.

fondest thoughts,

jeremy.

Life's but a walking shadow, a poor player
That struts and frets his hour upon the stage,
And then is heard no more: it is a tale
Told by an idiot, full of sound and fury,
Signifying nothing.

- *Macbeth*: Act V Scene V.

For my dear teacher
and friend
Avital Ronell

My hands are tied
The billions shift from side to side
And the wars go on with brainwashed pride
For the love of God and our human rights
And all these things are swept aside
By bloody hands time can't deny
And are washed away by your genocide
And history hides the lies of our civil wars

- Slash, McKagen, Rose: *Civil War*

The Spectacle of Terror: the Terror of the Spectacle

Without warning, next month, there will be explosions.

Some time in November or December, bomb blasts will be heard in as many as four MRT [Mass Rapid Transit: the state subway system] stations here. The Ministry of Home Affairs wants to know how well-prepared Singaporeans are if terrorists strike and, unlike other SCDF [Singapore Civil Defence Force] exercises, Singaporeans won't have a choice as to whether or not they want to take part.

There will be no warning, no schedule. If you happen to be a commuter at the selected stations – and the exercise is likely to take place during peak hours – Deputy Prime Minister Wong Kan Seng is waiting to see how ready you are.[1]

In many ways "we learned a lot from the night of the billowing cloud. But there is no substitute for a planned simulation."[2] This announcement might as well have come from the Voice of Fate[3] or Osama bin Laden. It would make absolutely no difference. For the state of terror knows no sources – it spins along its own axis; it is its own pure simulacrum. It does not even matter if Osama bin Laden exists or not – perhaps in some sense, Osama is always already dead and we have always known that: in fact we would rather have the spectre of bin Laden; in that way we can continue blaming him (without any consideration as to whether it is even possible for him to be involved in it). We might soon even want to consider blaming him for natural disasters.

Bomb blasts that are only heard: that is the fulfillment of the full potential of terrorism: a bomb blast that does not kill, but generates the full impact of a bomb blast. This is the utter and complete recognition of the realm of terror; that it exists only in the realm of representation. A bomb that kills is violent. A bomb that simulates is terrifying.

Both Deputy Prime Minister Wong and Osama bin Laden share this understanding.[4]

This is captured in the very statement that is bandied around without much consideration these days: "state of terror." Terror lies in a state. And not just a state in the sense of a geographical boundary with its laws and rules, but more precisely in a frame that has been set: this is exactly the same question of whether art exists without the frame. It is not so much whether it is the frame that makes it a work of art or not (what does it matter either way – are they even separable to

---

[1] Teo Hwee Nak. "Without warning, next month, there will be explosions." (October 2, 2005). *Weekend TODAY.* [parentheses my addition]

[2] Don Delillo. (1999). *White Noise.* pp.196.

[3] Flickers of Alan Moore & David Lloyd. (1995). *V for Vendetta.*

[4] The same can not be said of either Bush or Blair. It is this complete lack of comprehension of terror that has lead to actual wars still taking place: Afghanistan and Iraq are symptoms of this lack.

begin with) but the fact that the frame itself is a requirement.[5] In this manner, once the frame has been set, terror resides: there is no terror that is possible without this frame.

Terror only exists in the gap between the frame and the viewer.[6]

New(s). A stress on the new-ness of the news. Or perhaps the only factor in the consideration of what enters the specific realm that is news. Which is the impossible if we even consider taking Umberto Eco slightly seriously – after all, "what is new is old." But then in this realm, the one of news, Eco would have been completely missing the point; his statement pre-supposes there is a difference, perhaps in the form of transience, between new and old.[7] In fact, a consideration of news in terms of the new-ness is always already completely missing the point – news by definition is always completely new. It is a pure impossibility for news to be old; in this sense, the phrase 'old news' is purely ironic. For sans original, the copy is infinitely re-producible. The aura is not lost – for this would pre-suppose that it could be found somewhere; Benjamin would claim in the original.[8] The aura is always already found in the re-production – for the perfect re-production, the simulacra, is the perfect tension point between the (n)either lost (n)or found of this irreducible aura.

The original[9] that we all cling onto with desperation – the event that the news claims to make a link to – is based on a pre-supposition that there is a link, no matter how faint, between the event and the news; which is in essence the link

---

[5] This is akin to the issue of the signifier and the signified. Considering that we are born into signification, then despite our differing perspectives the signifiers remain socially constructed – hence we are always already caught by language on a denotative level. But this misses the point completely as a signifier and the signified are inseparable. In this sense, when the signified is altered (no matter how minutely) the entire sign is always already altered.

This is the very basis of the possibility of freedom: something that is the same but always already slightly different: for this is what allows a moment of subjectivity, a moment of difference that is found with repetition, within the same.

[6] This is an echo of Slavoj Zizek's comment "art only resides in the gap between the frame and the viewer," which was uttered at a Summer Seminar of the European Graduate School, August 2004.

[7] Then again, Eco could have been right on the mark for when we consider that 'what is new is old', what is old is also new which suggests that there is absolutely no difference between the old and the new in the first place – or that new and old are irreducibly different and have nothing to do with each other at all and hence are always already completely separated.

[8] Walter Benjamin. (1968). "The Work of Art in the Age of Mechanical Reproduction."

The Benjaminian aura that surrounds the original work requires an original in order to exist. Since news has no original referent – the event is always already completely separate from its representation that is news – the aura can never be found (unless you want to posit that it resides in the event but that has nothing to do with the news).

Perhaps a more interesting consideration would be that since there is no referent, news is always already original. In that case, an aura always surrounds all news. A simulated original, or an original simulacrum, mayhaps. This is the seductive effect of the news.

[9] For sans 'original' – or at least the concept of it even if we no longer believe in such a thing – the concept of surplus value cannot exist. For what surplus can you be generating from perfect copies? The only generation that is taking place is multiplications of the same thing: this problematizes the very legitimization of production itself (Lyotard), which is precisely the very nature of capitalism.

between the representation and the Real. In fact, the greater one is suspicious of the link between the event and the news, the greater the myth of the link itself is re-enforced. For the more one attempts to examine the inaccuracies of news (it can only be inaccurate if there is an original to match it against), even if the aim is to debunk news –mayhaps especially if it aims to debunk for that would require an even greater belief that there lies a truth beneath the surface - the more it serves to strengthen the pre-supposition that the news and the event have a connection.

An event: an occurrence that happens within a time and space: it is after all the material reality of the occurrence that confers on it the status of an event. Hence the effects of an event are felt only by the participants that have a material existence present at that point in time.[10]

News: a representation of the event: through language. Or, more accurately, through langue itself – for there is no distinction between the manifestations of langue: this is a structural concern and not so much one where there is a distinction between visual and textual representation (for that would once again fall into the trap of comparison and verification; the lure of representation itself – the seduction of the reader). It is the very act of re-presentation that permanently and totally divorces news from the event – for now we are treading into the realm of mediation.[11]

And it is this mediation that is the gap.[12]

***

From event to news. From event to representation. From an occurrence within a time and space to one which transcends time and space. The point at which a phenomenon enters the realm of metaphysics.

This is the very thing that is at stake here: singularity. The game of metaphysics is the game of capital – a wrenching out of time and space and a flattening of differences into a complete transparency. The transparency that is so revered modern society (the discourse of every modern state calls for greater transparency in the system under the discourse of accountability): this is the discourse of capital itself. With transparency there is nothing hidden – there is no longer a secret, everything is out in the open. And when everything can be seen, all can be ac-counted: it is this calculability that is the key, the measurability and the exchangeability, that is the hinge of capital.

---

[10] For only if one was actually in New York at 0900 on 11 September 2001, would one have an actual idea of why the two towers of the World Trade Centre are no longer standing. For the rest of us, it is mere faith – which is by definition blind – that there were two planes in the sky that crashed into them.

Not that it really matters for even if it were actually a humming bird, who would believe you anymore? And in a perverse way, they would not be wrong to call you a liar; truth lies in the realm of the news and it its networks – the world merely reconfirms what happens in the news. Reality television is an oxymoron – TV is real.

[11] An interesting consideration would be whether mediation is the complete break from material reality, as in the sense of the re-presentation (news in this case) having nothing to do with the event (so then news is a reality and the event is an unknowable Real as Lacan posits), or perhaps more radically, if the re-presentation is another material reality in itself (news is real, who cares about the event).

[12] This is the simulacra as Lucretius posits: the skin – the gap – the mediation. But it is this skin that becomes everything – this is the medium becoming the message.

And it is this transparency that is truly and profoundly evil.

***

It is completely impossible to differentiate the mediated from the original (assuming we are still clinging on to this idea). Consider the situation of Jean Charles de Menezes (he was shot to death in the London subway on the premise that he was potentially a 'suicide bomber'). The London police shot Menezes because he was displaying the signs of a suicide bomber – big back-pack, ran when he saw them, etc. In a perverse manner, his death was even more gruesome than those of actual suicide bomber (pinned down then executed at point blank range), because he did the unthinkable; attack the reality principle itself. By displaying the signs of a 'suicide bomber' whilst not actually being one, Menezes displayed for everyone the impossibility of differentiating between the two which calls into question the entire premise of homeland security (or even of the police) itself. For this then exposes what the law really is: a sign system to which one has to perform to. It is a crime to not display the correct signs in front of the law (what we commonly refer to as 'breaking the law') but it is true transgression when one exposes the true nature of the law itself: this is the reason for Menezes' execution.

One is never punished as severely if one merely breaks the law: law-breakers are what the law needs to justify its own existence: Prometheus is crucial to Zeus, as is Lucifer to God. One is punished with the utmost severity when one exposes the perverse core of the law itself. For instance, challenging capital punishment on grounds of morality, humanity, etc will be ignored by the state. Showing that capital punishment is the perverse core of the law "murder is illegal" will definitely get you into trouble. What you have done here is to show that the law cannot hold itself up – a rule can do everything except take itself seriously. Which is the reason why Pope Julius II is the ruler that the Catholic Church attempts to avoid mentioning: by selling 'indulgences', he showed that he was the only one who truly understood (and took seriously) Catholicism.

In fact a bomb hoax can cause more terror than an actual bomb threat (or even a bomb blast).[13] For the fear caused by a real bomb is diffusible, when it either is found, or at the point in which it explodes. In either situation, there is a definite end to the event. But in the case of a bomb hoax, there is no end: one can never be sure whether a hoax is really a hoax or not. In that manner, the bomb continually lies dormant – it will always explode at the next moment, or more radically, it has always already exploded and we are merely waiting for the effects to catch up.

Net-work games

It is this divorce with the Real (or perfect merging if you prefer) that allows news to enter the reality of the viewer. In this sense, it is not so much the desert of the real, but that the desert is real: the vastness and the emptiness of the sign is what allows the news to suture us into the reality of news itself.

---

[13] Any doubt of the power of hoaxes was removed in 1938 with Orson Welles' radio broadcast of *War of the Worlds*.

This is how the 'Stockholm effect' is playing out: it is not so much that the hostages in the event establish a relationship with the hostage takers anymore (even if they still continue to do so, it is no more of interest to us especially when we consider that there are just about no more hostages that are taken anymore) but that we are now all hostages in and through the media(tion). This is how terror sutures us through the television screen: you do not watch an event playing out on television – you are now playing out the event IN the television screen.

Perhaps the media works as they are "simulators of proximity."[14] TV, the Web, even newspapers and the like simulate the event into the consciousness of the reader such that the reader feels that (s)he is part of the event itself. In this manner, the medium is no longer separate from the participants in the exchange – the medium is very much a part of this exchange. This is when Marshall McLuhan is completely correct when he says that "the medium is the message,"[15] except that he does not realize just how apt his claim was: it is no mere metaphor nor is the media merely an extension of yourself. In this regard, it is Wolfgang Schirmacher who brings McLuhan to his full potential by showing how it is not us who use the media but it is the media who transforms us (I would even go as far as to say trans-figures us) – we are always already artificial beings, we are mediated beings.[16]

This brings us back to the idea of presence (simulated or otherwise, the concept still haunts us) – the idea of the center and of the logos; the need to establish an absolute through a meta-narrative. Through this simulated closeness, the reader can then decide on the credibility of the journalist, the accuracy of the text; in some sense the closer the reader feels to the event, or the Object if you prefer, the more accurate the representation seems to be. The game of finding and keeping the centre – the source of power – is on[17]: almost a physical centre this time, the centering of the reader within the text itself; a merging of sorts, or at least a blurring of boundaries taking place. Perhaps even a case of the reader reading herself; a perceived interpretation into which reality is spun. We might go as far as to say that the reader becomes the journalist that has written the paper: an extreme game of collapsing the binaries, the implosion of the author-reader dichotomy here. We have long already seen the poles of fact and fiction collapse. In some way, fiction precedes fact sometimes: how else do we explain Bill Nighly's rendition of 'Christmas is All Around Us' being in the running for Christmas song of the year in 2003.[18]

---

[14] Paul Virilio. (2002). *Ground Zero*. pp.41.

[15] Marshall McLuhan & Quentin Fiore. (1967). *The Medium is the Massage: An Inventory of Effects.*

[16] Wolfgang Schirmacher thoughts on the Homo Generator, media, and artificial life were discussed in his summer seminar at the European Graduate School, August 2005.

Perhaps the question that arises here is whether the mediated being is an artificial being, in the sense of whether there is a non-mediated being, to begin with. For everyone is always already perceived in and through oneself, which is not actually a solipsistic view because one's perception of oneself is always already mediated – the Lacanian 'mirror' has already taken care of that.

Are we then not resting on the indeterminacy of being (n)either natural (n)or artificial – constantly mediated in and through (n)either ourselves (n)or externalities.

[17] Johannes Fabian. (1983). *Time and the Other: How Anthropology makes its Object.*

[18] In the 2003 movie *Love Actually* (Richard Curtis, Dir.) Billy Mack (played by Bill Nighly) attempts to revive his career by releasing the Christmas tune, "Christmas is All Around Us," which was in the running for Christmas song of the year. In the weeks after the movie was released, the same song had a run in

Is proximity the very reason that 'live' broadcasts are so popular? We might go as far as saying that if a news broadcast is 'live' then suddenly there is an element of increased credibility (and popularity even). In that sense, the 1987 European cup match between Real Madrid and Napoli,[19] which took place in an empty stadium, retains the very presence of a match. The 'live' transmission allows us to catch the purity of the image; we did not have to be there to be there. In some way perhaps this pure image allows us to be more a part of the match than being at the stadium itself; the eye of the camera – the 'live' feed – brings you closer to the match than your own eye could ever have.

But would not one be able to verify news by going back to an event itself? For one, the most common way in which we verify news is by checking with another news source – for instance, if one doubts news coverage on CNN, one might check with the BBC or FOX. However this merely amounts to verifying representation via representation. More interestingly, verification would be an impossibility: the event is always already past, occurring within a specific time and space: once past, it is irretrievable.   Which does not actually negate the issue of verification itself: verification needs not a relation with an absolute Other: verification always already legitimizes itself in and through itself.

News exists in and through itself. The truth of news is that news establishes truths and verifies truths in and through news: a pure Actant-Network as conceptualized by Bruno Latour at play: truth is established by its position with reference to other established truths within the structure of a discourse.[20]

The event is no longer necessary – news is completely independent of the event. For if this were not the case, public relations would be a completely non-existent entity; bomb hoaxes (which are essentially the same as PR[21] acts: the creation of news out of a pseudo-event: in essence in the absence of an event) would not be possible. In fact, an event merely hampers news; sans event, news is completely limitless – an actual bomb can be defused; a hoax on the other hand has no beginning and hence no end.

---

the UK charts and was in contention for the very same award. This would not be quite so unusual if not for the fact that in the movie, Mack admits that the song is merely a hack job – a re-hash of an old hit that was done for the sole purpose of reviving a dead career. In this instance, it has transposed a fictional music career into the realm of reality. Billy Mack, meet Bill Nighly: who ever said we could tell them apart to begin with.

[19] Real Madrid vs Napoli [16.09.1987]. The match was played in an empty stadium as part of a UEFA punishment on Real Madrid for crowd trouble. It was televised 'live.'

[20] In Bruno Latour's Actant-Network, networks are not so much mere structures for the transmission of information but rather engage in the very nature of the exchange itself. Hence the network – for instance a network of humans that are exchanging some form of information – is itself affected and altered by the exchange – the network itself is live and dynamic.

[21] This is the secret of public relations: there is no public to begin with – there is only a mass. The public is narrated into existence and then a relationship is created between the organization and a simulated public, after-which the public 'responds' to the message of the organization: a perfect circle and a never-ending cycle. This is the playing out of the society of consumption. But in an even more radical sense, the consumers are simulated and it is reality itself that is consumed.

It is in this light that the truth of news comes to the fore – news operates in the realm of the symbolic, using its own currency of exchange; a pure system of exchange.

(In) The Realm of the Senses[22]

News: the paradox of truth where the impossibility of representation is the very condition for the seduction of the reader: into the game of meaning – the lure of the signified proving irresistible.

In the realm of the symbolic, there is a permanent and never-ending exchange of signs: a constant ecstasy of communication where the entire point of communication is communication itself: an exchange that hinges on the complete lack of depth of the sign itself – the empty signifier. This is the secret of news, its perverse core that must never be revealed.

The empty signifier is the only guarantee that the news is never devoid of an audience. For there will never be a lack of a signified – in fact, the very opposite would occur – there is always an excess of the signified at play. The empty signifier ensures that the perfect sign – a master-signifier onto which everything can be attached – is in place such that news will always remain completely and utterly meaningless.

This is precisely the seduction of the reader: the reader will always already be part of the news itself, constantly giving it meaning which ensures that the concept of news not having an audience is an impossibility: and in fact, the greater the reader searches for depth in news (that is the search for meaning), the greater the seduction of news. In this sense, all traditional forms of resistance to the mass media – media literacy, mass media studies, visual literacy, and the like – are all doomed from the beginning to failure. In fact, what they are doing is propagating the seduction to an even greater extent (once again, searching for inaccuracies and paradoxes only strengthens the myth that there is a meaning, a depth, to this entire game in the first place).

This is the secret of the news: that it is founded on nothing – but it is this nothingness that allows the readers to suck themselves into the news, by giving it some form of meaning. News can – in the terms of the perfect seductress – 'be whatever you want me to be.' And every attempt to bridge that gap, by attempting to search for the meaning within the news, is always already the production of meaning not of the news, but for news – the effect of which is simply, more news.

***

Terror resides in the realm of news, a realm which is founded on nothing – a representation sans Object (for even if there is an Object, it is not actually necessary). The term 'news event' is tautological: news is an event: more

---

[22] Is the name Empire of the Senses (L'Empire des Sens) more appropriate in some way? For is one ever in control of the senses – in the sense of a Being-in-itself experiencing stimuli – or perhaps the senses are what shapes a Being: the senses lord over a Being – the senses are the empire that a Being responds to. Not that it is a dichotomy in any way whatsoever: in this sense, perhaps the senses are the empire that a Being responds with then.

accurately, news is the event. Not only is there no event sans news – in this realm there are no more events.

The event as a pure exchange of signs: a pure circulation of signs: the Real as an orgasm in the ecstasy of exchangeability.

Metaphysics is when metaphors become real[23]

It is in this game of circulating signs that terror resides, and in many cases nowadays, (p)resides. For it is via this channel (the very button that you press or the paper that you pick up) that the reminders of constant danger reach you: just take a ride on any subway in the world and hear the constant reminders of 'suspicious baggage', or better still go to an airport. The constant changing of the "Alert levels" in the United States is symptomatic of this ubiquity of terror (in this case, the changing is the key – what the actual alert level is, is never the point. The fact that it changes constantly reminds people that something is actually happening: this is the simulated dynamism of terror). It seems like anyone carrying a backpack is now a reminder of the possibility of bombings.

It is not so much that the discourse of terror has seeps into our lives but more so that our lives are now the discourse of terror: if backpacks are now a sign of terror, but the signifier still remains the same, then clearly the signified has changed. It is the utter inability to distinguish a metaphor from reality that leads to signs at airports such as, "jokes about hijacking planes are not funny. It is a Federal Offence and you will be prosecuted."[24] More radically, it is not that we are unable to distinguish any longer, but that there is no longer anything to distinguish.

It is this indistinguishability – this loss of all metaphor, all irony – that has allowed the spectre of Osama bin Laden to haunt us: it matters not if the man is alive or not. In fact, it is the proverbial 'nine lives' that bin Laden is living but this is of absolutely no consequence for the name has overtaken the man already. Jesus has proven that killing a man can bring a name to immortality: the name Osama bin Laden is operating on the same logic – from signifiers referring to flesh, both of their names have been transfigured into brands. This branding is very apparent at every site of violence: the moment the bombs went off in Bali (in both 2003 and 2005) the name that surfaced was Jemaah Islamiah (the alleged South-East Asian wing of Al Qaeda); the same pattern surfaced in London, Madrid and so on. In fact, from September 12 2001, Al Qaeda has become a new signifier for bombings.

---

[23] It was Jean-Francois Lyotard who uttered this in the film *Lyotard/ signature*. (1996). [Janina Quint, Dir.].

[24] Which then makes joking and assassinating a President of the United States reside on the same scale (where else but in the US could such a sign exist). In some way this is a profound recognition that the President is merely another metaphor: the masses vote for an image and from that moment on, there is power vested in that image – power that can send real people to their deaths: a simulated President, a simulated war based on simulated reasons with very real consequences.

For whom does this bell toll?

Considering that most of the signs of terror reach us through the mass media (much of which directly or indirectly still come under the auspices of the state), the question that arises is, why are they still in mass(ive) circulation? Although one can argue that many of the messages from bin Laden and Al Qaeda come from themselves (for this moment, let us suspend disbelief questions of their existence), the question remains of how many of us have direct access to them? Even if one brings up the issue of the Internet and how content is free, one must always remember that access to the internet is not: control is exerted not in realm of content (say whatever you want to) but via infrastructure (but no one will ever hear it).[25]

One question that arises is: is the circulation of the signs of terror a tactic of the very system that is attempting to combat it? Is the sign of terror a tactic of the modern state: is terror written into the very fabric of the state? For sure, the immediate result in the modern state after September 11 (one can now use the date as a signifier: the signified has been locked in forever: even the year does not need to be stated anymore: time was arrested and sucked into that very instant: every other year has lost that date to 2001) was the 'sacrifice' of civil liberties. The 'Patriot Act' of Bush's United States is not an anomaly: it has manifested itself in various ways everywhere (in many ways, the 'Patriot Act' is a resurrection of the British 'Internal Security Act' that was imposed on all its colonies. Many of the colonies retained this act after independence as a convenient tool of control of their subjects). In fact, states have co-opted the word 'terrorist' as a label to be used on anyone whom they deem to be an 'enemy' – all that is missing from the label is an armband (in some way, perhaps no armband is necessary anymore as there is no longer a need for obvious signs – labels are now internal: this is the embodiment of ideology taking place).

In some sense, the discourse on terror works as an Ideological State Apparatus in order that the Repressive State Apparatuses can be created. Even though no one truly believes that ISAs work any longer (perhaps this is a true sign of their triumph) the ISAs set the condition for the RSAs to be established.[26]

Consider the invasion of Iraq. In deposing of Saddam Hussein, the US has removed a figure that has never really been truly opposed to them. In this sense they may have ensured that Saddam's successor will be a true enemy of the US – Jalal Talabani does not count as he is a mere figurehead; in many ways he is playing exactly the same role as Saddam. When the true enemy of the US comes to power in Iraq (which the appointment of Talabani will more of less ensure) – what better way to get a true enemy elected than to install a puppet: clearly the lessons of Ngo Dinh Diem are being put into practice here – we may begin to see the real attacks on the US. Perversely Bush Jr. may have been prophetic when he accused Iraq of being the perpetrators of attacks on the US.

---

[25] For a more comprehensive argument on this, please see Korinna Patelis. (1999). "The Political Economy of the Internet."

[26] 'Ideological' and 'Repressive State Apparatuses' are taken from Louis Althusser. (1977). "Ideology and the State." In fact, as Althusser aptly notes, you know ideology is working at the point when "history becomes nature."

One reading of this would be that it is a failure of US foreign policy in that they are introducing a greater (and even real) problem for the future. But it is even more interesting if we consider the possibility that the US always already knew this. In this manner, the current occupation of Iraq is the provocation needed to discover the True enemy as this would provide the very conditions that are needed for the disciplining of their own subjects.[27] Even more than creating the very conditions for control of the subjects in the state, the discourse of terror is the very hinge on which the concept of the state rests upon. For through terror, the nation is narrated into existence: this occurs through the creation of the Other (which the state craves for – this is what it feeds on; sans the Other, the state will wither away).[28] Globalization has created not so much a "global village" as McLuhan terms it, but rather a "global metropolis,"[29] where there is a commonality between people, but a commonality sans singularity: in a metropolis everyone is living in the same space (and this space is now sans frontier) but no one knows anyone else; in effect there are no more persons; there is only a mass. In this "global metropolis", there is only a flattening of differences – this is precisely the condition that is needed for exchange to occur – which is also the condition in which the state fails to function.[30] In this manner, globalization is driving the state into oblivion: the state is quickly becoming an obsolete concept. A good indication of this was the creation of the European Union – is the trend then headed towards the creation of an Asian Union, an African Union and after that maybe a World Union? With the concept of the state in peril, is the discourse of terror then an attempt at re-territorialization: the creation of an Other (the enemy) in order that the state can once again narrate itself into existence. We see Australia do this after each bomb attack in Bali – both times they have claimed that Australians were the 'targets'[31] of these bombs and this has drawn the nation 'together'. This discourse has also clearly worked in the United States after September 11; never had the nation been as united as on the 12th.

The narration of the nation only works with the creation of an Other, which then draws everyone together against them. This was the genius of Hitler: drawing the historically neglected class, the middle class, together through the creation of the

---

[27] This paragraph owes a great debt to Slavoj Zizek. (2004). "The Iraq War: Where is the True Danger." The article can be found at http://www.lacan.com/iraq.htm

[28] It is only at this point, the point of no Other, that the Communist state can exist. In essence it is a state without state – the withering away of the state occurs when the dictatorship of the proletariat negate themselves; in essence this is what is meant by the second negation – the first is the negation of the bourgeoisie, the second is the negation of the Other (and hence the Self as well).

[29] I owe this term to Ong Siow Heng. (8 August, 2000). Open lecture at the School of Communication and Information: Singapore.

[30] For instance, India only exists in and through a difference with Pakistan (and all other states in the world). At the moment, most Indians do not believe in the concept of India any longer – their identification comes not from the state of India but from the various states that they live in (and languages they speak). In fact, the only time that Indians view themselves as a nation is during a cricket match: this may well be the reason that cricket is always kept on the front page of news.

[31] "The terrorist attacks against the Australian Embassy in Jakarta on 9 September 2004 and in Bali on 12 October 2002 underscore the ongoing threat posed by terrorists to Australians overseas. Australians are directly threatened by terrorism. Australia and Australians have been specifically named by international terrorist groups, including Osama bin Laden and his Al-Qa'ida network and Jemaah Islamiyah, as a legitimate target of attack."

Official statement of the Australian Department of Foreign Affairs and Trade as of October 17, 2005. Found at http://www.smartraveller.gov.au/zw-cgi/view/Advice/General

Other in the Jewish people.[32] The enemy is a necessity for a disaster (bomb blasts and plane crashes do fall into the realm of disasters as well) sans an enemy does not work: just look at the reactions of the US after the New Orleans fiasco following Hurricane Katrina.

In this sense, has the state co-opted the discourse of terror in order to ensure its own existence? Or more interestingly, perhaps we might want to consider if they are actually part of the same discourse to begin with.

Spirits ... Ghosts ... Hauntings ...

The spectre of communism has been exorcised: as has the spectre of revolutions. There is a new spirit that haunts us – the spirit of terror – a spirit that invades and infects – but a spirit which comes from both everywhere and nowhere at the same time- mayhaps this is the true source of the horror – the ghost that cannot be exorcised, for there is no body to exhume in the first place.

It was at the Last Supper that the power of the corpse-less corpse was revealed. For the Twelve consumed his body even as he was alive: there was absolutely no need for a cadaver in order that the entire mystery of Christianity takes place. It is Islam that recognizes the pointless-ness of the death on the cross (and even the resurrection): Isa goes straight to heaven (his movement from human to divine does not require death). At every utterance of "Corpus Christi," we are reminded to "do this in memory of me" – the focus is on re-membering Jesus. It is at this moment that the trans-figuration occurs, for memory can never be of the dead; those we re-member are always already brought back to life.[33]

It is our re-membering that breathes life into it: like the phoenix that rises from the ashes: for whilst in memory the subject is always alive, in order to be remembered, one must always already be dead: it is in the process of remembering that one is brought back to life. It is through this re-membering that we play at being necromancers.

Terror: the corpse-less corpse: forever (un)dead: infinitely (brought) alive.

It is clearly not the violence that fascinates us. For even hoaxes hold our attention (they always seem particularly attractive to us). Nor can it be the actual number of people who are affected by the event itself (for one moment, let us suspend disbelief at representation and allow ourselves to imagine that the representation and the event have a connection). The actual numbers killed are never actually that high. But then again, perhaps the very fascination with numbers is due to the fact that there is no association with reality. When Stalin proclaimed, "the death of millions is a statistic," perhaps he was not being radical enough: considering that one can only die for oneself – death is experienced by yourself and no one else, no one can die for you nor experience it with you – all death is only a statistic. Perhaps then it is death that calls out to us from this indiscernible void – death that is unknown and unknowable, and that we desperately try to understand

---

[32] It was Siegfried Zielinski who pointed out the genius of Hitler in directing his discourse towards the oft neglected middle class: historically all revolutions are directed either at the ruling or the proletariats. Zielinski's comments came as part of a summer seminar at the European Graduate School, August 2005.

[33] This paragraph owes a debt to a conversation with Jason Ng. (18 October, 2005): Singapore.

via this spewing up of numbers (there is no better sign of incomprehensibility than a random throwing out of figures – just look at the amount of statistics that keep showing up at elections).

Death: and a small death. But terror works not so much as an orgasmic moment – the moment in which the Real enters reality which is why it shocks us so (as many have posited) – but rather as the forever delayed orgasm.

Terrorism: an attempt at the eternal distancing from the orgasm of totality that is globalization. Terrorism is the refusal of globalization to accept the complete and total flattening out that globalization itself entails: this flattening out, the very conditions of total exchangeability, would be the complete and utter triumph of the logic of the capital. But every system dreams of its own failure – it cannot endure its complete triumph. For the total triumph of capitalism would also be its own collapse as no system can endure its own completion, no logic can sustain itself in its logical extreme. The fantasy of capital – complete exchangeability – requires a gap (an incompleteness which never can be bridged) in order to sustain itself: if the fantasy was fulfilled, this would be the point at which the Real would over-whelm us. For instance the fantasy of the disciplinary system – as set out by Michel Foucault – is for the complete and utter obedience of the subject. But if that were to happen, the system itself would collapse – Foucault's dispositifs assume the fundamental resistance of the subject to control mechanisms. Sans this resistance, the dispositif itself crumbles: what good would jails be if everyone did not mind being in them to begin with? Terrorism itself is the very gap that allows for the jouissance of globalization to continue: it is the gap that is crucial and it is terrorism that is fulfils this role.[34]

Terrorism: the ghost of globalization: the spirit that continues to haunt globalization from within; both its possessor and its guardian angel: from within, for what else is now capable of stopping globalization from reaching its own conclusion – fulfilling its complete potential – but itself.

***

Lenin announced the death of revolution when he uttered the question, "what is to be done?" In that statement, he was unaware of his prophecy: for it is the attempt to answer this question that dooms all revolutions to failure. The question itself pre-supposes an objective (the 'what' to be done), and a methodology (the 'how' this is to be done): the result of this is a measurement, that is, a calculation of how 'successful' the revolution was. It is this which sets the very conditions for a reproducibility of the revolution. Hence the logic of revolution ends up being exactly the same as that of the system which it claims to be revolting against.

In fact, all revolutions are paralogical by nature. In the creation of dissensus within the system, all they serve to do is to hone the system to ensure that it runs at maximum performativity.[35] The very term revolution itself gives its nature away – there is an inevitable circularity that all revolutions are doomed to from the very beginning. In this circuitry, there is no hope for anything new; only the widening

---

[34] This paragraph owes a great debt to Jean Baudrillard. (2002). *The Spirit of Terrorism.*

[35] The terms "paralogy," "dissensus," and "maximum performativity," are used in the sense of Jean-Francois Lyotard. (1984). *The Postmodern Condition.*

and expansion of the circle itself and the production – this is always the key – of a new-ishness; this is the surplus value that drives the system itself. This is precisely what is shown in the movie *The Matrix*.[36] The role of Zion was that of a virus – one that had been implanted by the System itself – in fact, each re-generation of the Matrix, a Zion is always programmed into the system. This was the dissensus that the Matrix had to continually battle against in order that it functioned at maximum capability. In this sense, it was Neo that was the ultimate agent of the Matrix. This was exactly the same role that was played to perfection by Martin Luther: in his protest of the excesses of the Church, he re-inscribed God back into religion; for one can only protest that the Church had forgotten God in its practices if there was still a God to believe in. In this sense, Luther was the greatest agent of the Catholic Church – it was the Protestant movement that resurrected the God that Catholicism had murdered (or had at least hidden away behind images).

***

In fulfilling the condition of the gap in order that the fantasy of globalization will never be fulfilled, terrorism is ensuring the very survival of globalization itself. Perhaps the true fantasy of globalization (and any other system of thought or logic) is that it is in a permanent inability to fulfill itself – a constant reaching towards the orgasm without ever reaching the point of the little, let alone the real, death.

> Whenever exchange is impossible, what we encounter is terror. Any radical otherness at all is thus the epicenter of terror: the terror that such otherness holds, by virtue of its very existence for the normal world. And the terror that this world exercises upon the otherness in order to annihilate it.[37]

It is over radical otherness that the war of terror is waged. Each side – the state, the Subject, and the image (yes even the image is not spared, for this war knows no boundaries: there is no longer a difference, or differentiability to be more precise, between simulation and reality any longer: "the simulacra is true" now does exist in Ecclesiastes: or more radically still, there is no longer a simulacra; there is only the true) are all fighting for their very survival.

The existence of all parties is on the line: and Otherness is the very stake on which this game is played.[38]

---

[36] Joel Silver. (Producer). Andy Wachowski & Larry Wachowski. (Directors). (1999). *The Matrix.*

[37] Jean Baudrillard. (1993). "The Melodrama of Differences" in *The Transparency of Evil.* pp.128.

[38] It is a stake in the very precise sense, for this game is one of challenge, where the stakes continually rise. There is nothing more to it than the game itself a game of who dares to be more Other than the other. In fact, in this vampiric game (we must never forget that the stake is also deadly and can destroy eternity in an instant) that seduces all the parties, what we are playing for is Singularity (long lost in this game of equalization and flattening), the ghost of Singularity that refuses to die.

Reading. Interpretation. (Re)Writing

> The dead letter of writing often has much more influence that the living word. A letter is a secretive communication; one is master of the situation, feels no pressure from anyone's actual presence, and I do believe a young girl would prefer to be all alone with her ideal, that is, at certain moments, and precisely at those moments, when it has the strongest effect on her mind. Even if her ideal has found an ever so perfect expression in a particular beloved object, there nevertheless are moments when she feels that in the ideal there is a vastness that the actuality does not have.

> In this letters are an aid; they help one to be invisibly and mentally present in these moments of sacred dedication, while the idea that the actual person is the author of the letter forms a natural and easy transition to the actuality.[1]

The evoking of the dead: and the rising of meaning. Is this "vastness" that she feels, the resurrection of the phoenix from the ashes: when we are reading (a text into existence), is this the moment in which we are all necromancers?

We must never forget that in that "vastness" lies a void – an emptiness that we are sucked into. This is the secret of the letter – the appearance of the meaning is also always at the same time its dis-appearance: (n)either an unfolding (n)or a folding but always already both at the same time. But herein lies the moment of its "sacred dedication" – in order for meaning to (a)rise from the "dead letter," there is a sacrifice and this takes the form of multiplicity (or to be more exact, the potentiality of multiplicity). For in order for any meaning to arise, the potentiality of all the other possibilities must remain unfulfilled: they are sacrificed in order that one (of the possible) meanings enters into the realm of actuality. The sacrifice is not of the order of a negative in the sense of a failure of potentiality (when something is not actualized), for potentiality only exists when there is a aspect of non-potentiality,[2] but rather that it is in the fulfillment of their full potentiality (through non-potentiality) of the multiple possibilities that one of them is transfigured into the realm of actuality.

How and why this actuality occurs remains as mystery, as terrifying as that is (for it is not truly a mystery if it does not terrify us, make us tremble). We tremble each and every time meaning arises because at every instance of its appearance, there is a reminder and a recollection of death. This is the magnitude of the sacrifice: the death of the multiplicity of possibilities (in their fulfillment of non-potentiality), in order that one may arise from its ashes.

And it is this death that grants it its "vastness," which has the "strongest effects on [our] mind." For it is singularity that scares us, makes us tremble. Not so much that there is a singular meaning that arises, for this always questionable (and in some ways perhaps an impossibility), but the fact that this resurrection always occurs in fidelity to singularity. And it is this ghost of the singular that continues to

---

[1] Soren Kierkegaard. (1997). *The Seducer's Diary*. pp.158-159.

[2] For a more comprehensive meditation on potentiality, please see Giorgio Agamben. (1999). *Potentialities: Collected Essays in Philosophy.*

haunt us, the spectre that refuses to be exorcised in this time of universality, in this time of flatness.

But perhaps in order to meditate on this particular resurrection, we have to take a little detour.

***

If terror resides in the media space then how does it affect us: the question of whether or not it affects us is a moot one, for it clearly does: there is no denying the ubiquity of terror – it practically governs our daily lives.

Here we have to first begin by considering 'governs' in its literal sense, for the very people who limit our civil liberties (and this is one of the direct and most obvious effects of terror that we see) are the very people that we put in office in the first place. This is not just the paradox of democracy at play, in the sense that democracy guarantees the unhappiness of a minority (the elections being a tyranny of the majority) for the logic of democracy itself guarantees unhappiness due to a lack of freedom for everyone.

In a Fascist state, the Subject is denied all freedom. All power lies in the hand of the one absolute leader – (s)he plays the role of the (absolute) Other, on which everything depends. The Subject is merely a part of the whole body (in the form of the state): this is the corporatization of the state and its subjects. All actions of the Subject is a result of the Leader – perversely this ensures the absolute freedom of the Subject; for there is absolutely nothing that the Subject can responsible for; (s)he is merely a cog in the entire body. Hence the Subject is not responsible for anything, even her/ him self. Even if the Subject is punished by the law for something in a Fascist state, it is not that (s)he is guilty for doing or not doing something (for one can only be guilty if one is responsible for it) but the fact that the Leader deems her/ him so. Due to the fact that the private and the public are collapsed (in Fascism there is either only a public sphere, or the spheres are indistinguishable, which amounts to the same thing), this ensures the true freedom of the Self (where one is accountable only to the Self and not to any external force). The moment when the Other attempts to swallow (and ingest) the Self is also the moment in which the Self is most free.[3]

In a Totalitarian state (the Soviet Union under Stalin for instance), the Other takes the form of the Party. In this manner, once again there is no freedom for the Subject as everything is done as directed by the Party; all responsibility comes under, and is of, the Party. Hence the Subject can always blame the Party for anything (even bad weather). Once again, a perverse form of freedom for the Subject can be found in this situation.

---

[3] This raises the question of the relation between freedom and responsibility. Can one only be absolutely free when one has no responsibility, when one has no Other to respond to (and with)? For sans the Other, this is the only time in which one is truly free to completely exercise one's will without considering the will of the Other. In any other case, the complete fulfillment of one's freedom brings along with it the effacement of the Other: this is the realm of the sadist.

This also raises the question of the Self: can the Self exist without responding to the Other (or even more pertinently, can the Self exist sans the Other)? But then, if the Other is always already known through the Self, is the Self then always already a simulated Self: literally a (mirror) image?

In a democracy, the Subject has to assume complete responsibility for both her/ his actions and also that of the state. The freedom of the Subject is closely related to the choices presented to her/ him, and in fact, the point of ultimate freedom (and choice) comes at the moment of election. At each election, the Subject has three options: elect a particular candidate or party, spoil the vote, or refuse to vote. But whichever option the Subject chooses, by definition (by virtue of the logic of 'social contract' to which the Subject is bound), (s)he has already agreed to accept the outcome of the election (which makes all claims to Bush's illegal election moot the moment the results were officially announced; one can challenge them up to the point which they are announced, but no longer after). More crucially, the Subject has to take responsibility for the outcome – in effect, whether or not you elected that particular person/ party, you are responsible for her/ his/ their actions. Which means that whatever legislation is passed by those elected to office – no matter how brutal or disagreeable they may be – is passed by the Subject on themselves.

This lack of freedom in democracy is due to the attempt of the Subject at bridging the gap between her/ him self and the Other. In claiming total freedom of choice, the Subject swallows the Other. But by doing this, the Subject does not rid her/ him self of the Other (this is an impossibility) but instead creates an(O)ther in her/ him self. This takes the form of the Law (which becomes an Absolute Law) which is what binds her/ him self.[4]

> When exactly can people be said to be happy? In a country like Czechoslovakia in the late 1970s and 1980s, in a way, people were, in a way, actually happy: three fundamental conditions of happiness were fulfilled. Their material needs were basically satisfied – not too satisfied, since the excess of consumption can in itself generate unhappiness. It is good to experience a brief shortage of some goods on the market from time to time (no coffee for a couple of days, then no beef, then no TV sets): these brief periods of shortage functioned as exceptions that reminded people that they should be glad that these goods were generally available – if everything is available all the time, people take this availability as an evident fact of life, and no longer appreciate their luck. So life went on in a regular and predictable way, without any great efforts or shocks; one was allowed to withdraw into one's private niche. A second extremely important feature: there was the Other (the Party) to blame for everything that went wrong, so that one did no feel really responsible – if there was a temporary shortage of some goods, even if stormy weather caused great damage, it was "their" fault. And last, but not least, there was an Other Place (the consumerist West) about which one was allowed to dream; and one could even visit it sometimes – this place was at just the right distance: not too far away, not too close, This fragile balance was disturbed – by what? By desire precisely. Desire was the force

---

[4] Asking 'what' the Subject is bound to is a moot question. There is no Object to which this binding takes place: the binding does not occur with an externality; it is an internal binding which the Subject binds her/ him self to. In effect, this is an Object-less binding that takes place: which makes it all the more inescapable: if there was an Object, the Subject can always devise a means of escape from it. An Object-less binding is always already inescapable – it is a perfect bind.

that compelled the people to move on – and end up in a system in which the great majority are definitely less happy.[5]

It is the desire to close this gap that leads to the nightmare situation: the logic of freedom only works until the point in which one gets to choose. For the freedom of choice is perfect only when it is not a real choice, that is when the guidelines have already been laid out and the consequences are not real. The nightmare begins when one begins to believe that one can really choose: in this manner, the outcome is never known (by definition) and it is at this point that the Real springs forth and stares into the face of the Subject. The desire for false choices is shown by the success of advertising: choose between the hundreds of different shaving creams; it matters not at all, for every one of them is the same (but your desire to choose has been satisfied; but more importantly, the gap still remains). In that case, the question that arises is why the Real does not over-take us at each election (since that is a choice)? This is simply because elections (and politics) have long ago entered the realm of simulated choice. This was best captured when the slogan "Join the Revolution" appeared on television screens in Singapore in mid-2005. This was probably the first 'revolutionary-like' comment ever seen on TV in the last 20 years, until it was revealed that it was an advertisement for instant noodles (Koka). But perhaps this is the very reflection on politics: it is nothing more than a sign system of exchange. One might as well be voting for Schroeder or Merkel, Bush or Kerry, Nissin or Maggi.[6]

The viewing of distances

When we consider the distance that is inherent in tele-vision, is it not the viewer, or more aptly the spectator (for does one merely look at television or is one always already a part of it?) the one that bridges the gap? In some way, it is the medium that brings us closer than ever before to the event (in the sense of what is occurring): this is the very concept of 'live' television; in many instances, the eye of the camera brings you closer to the action than if you were there yourself. But tele-vision in itself always already maintains that there is a distance to the event: this is apparent from its own name. In this manner, is it the medium which traverses the distance, or is it the spectator who does this her/ him self?

This opens up the consideration of whether it is tele-vision that sutures us or is it we who plunge ourselves into the screen in order to feel 'part' of the event: is it the viewer who transfigures her/ him self into a spectator?

It is this bridging of the gap between the viewer and the event that allows for this transfiguration into a third – the spectator – that makes one feel like a part of the event. It is precisely this transfiguration that allows meaning to be created: when the viewer feels like (s)he is a part of the event, that (s)he 'understands' the

[5] Slavoj Zizek. (2003). *The Puppet and the Dwarf: the Perverse Core of Christianity.* pp.42.

The above paragraphs on Fascism, Totalitarianism and Democracy were inspired by a conversation with Slavoj Zizek. (8 August, 2004): Saas Fee.

[6] The Koka 'Join the Revolution' advertisement was brought to my attention in a conversation with Serene Chua. (27 September, 2005): Singapore.

event, (s)he creates her/ his own meaning for the event. In effect, what (s)he has done is to write her/ his own event into existence.[7]

A new event: call it a pseudo-event if you wish, for in the strictest sense, an event can never be approached (or begun to be fully understood).

This is the true profundity of the statement "art lies in the gap between the frame and the viewer"[8]: meaning is created alongside the transfiguration into the spectator – meaning is that of the spectator.   But even in this process of transfiguration, one thing remains – the seeing, the Eye.

A question that is opened by this is: why do we trust what we see more than what we hear, touch, taste, or feel? This is very clearly shown in the saying "seeing is believing," which suggests that one must see in order that one believes. In fact, there is no other sense that stands on its own besides sight: all the other senses act as merely sources of confirmation or affirmation at best but there is no denying the privileging of the Eye.

Seeing. Being closer. In many ways there is a hint of presence that comes along with seeing – presence that has always been privileged over absence.[9] But is that not true of the other senses as well? It is not only seeing that brings one into the presence (or even essence) of the event. However, it is rather clear that it is sight that has been privileged over all the other senses when it comes to verification, when it comes to the matter of the truth, and of knowing what is true.[10] We see this manifested in the manner in which God is referred to – the All-Seeing who Knows everything: in some sense, God knows everything because (S)he sees everything (the Cao Dai religion in Vietnam distills the essence of God to perfection by representing Her with an Eye).

***

---

[7] The only time that this does not occur is when one allows for one's understanding to be in want of understanding, in the sense of allowing for an un-understanding – an inability to fully comprehend, and fully subsume under one's cognition – to be a part of understanding. It is this gap in understanding that allows for the event to remain a true event; an occurrence in a time and space that escapes (full) comprehension, and total subsumption.

For a meditation on the phrase "understanding is in want of understanding," please see Werner Hamacher. (1996). *Premises: Essays on Philosophy and Literature from Kant to Celan.* In particular, refer to the essay "Premises."

[8] Uttered by Slavoj Zizek at a Summer Seminar of the European Graduate School, August 2004.

[9] A comprehensive meditation of this can be found in Jacques Derrida. (1997). *On Grammatology.*

[10] In Wolfgang Schirmacher's conception, the privileging of sight has to do with the survival needs of humankind, in that sight was the only way (and maybe still is for even radar is a form of seeing) in which one can distinguish friend from foe. Schirmacher also contends that meta-physics is a tool for survival, for it pre-programs snap decisions (without any need for consideration) – a quick decision that can be trained a priori.

It is probably this snap decision that can be conditioned a priori, that has lead advertising to become increasingly visually lead: the industry is premised on as little complication as possible – if the consumer were given time to meditate, advertising would not have an effect: consumers would be purchasing based on the strength of the product itself (God forbid).

After the death of God, has television become the new all-seeing eye; the eye to which we turn to for truth?[11] Even when we attempt to verify the truth, we always verify one eye against another (in the form of the coverage on CNN against BBC against FOX) which merely legitimizes sight. Even the Internet is merely playing the role of Neo and Martin Luther: in bringing charges of inaccuracy against television (especially in the realm of news), the Internet merely solidifies the concept of truth and more importantly its relation with seeing (and the Eye). In effect the logic of representation (which is the logic of images and truth) is strengthened with each accusation of inaccuracy. After all, most of the charges via the Internet are still based on images.

There is much we can learn here from Ronald Reagan: after all his PR strategy was built around the concept that 'when the eye and the ear compete, the eye always wins.'[12] More recently, the Abu Gharib scandal was a challenge of the Image against the 'word' of the White House and the military – it was built around the photographs that were taken within the gulag itself. This incident merely confirmed the fact that it is sight (and the image) that is equated to (we are now beyond merely equating 'with' anymore: the equation has become absolute) truth. It is for this exact reason that both Bush administrations are so particular about where the camera crews can go during each of the Gulf Wars. The lesson of Vietnam has been learnt: it not so much that it is the television war, bur that wars are fought on television.

> When I went around campus informing people of a fellow college student that self-immolated in protest of the Vietnam War, a girl responded "No, it didn't happen. I didn't see it on TV."[13]

It is for this very reason that the war is won or lost on television: it is no longer about the numbers that perish: war is about winning the "hearts and souls" of the people – this is a rare occasion when Bush Jr. is right. And television, which brings us to the event and which allows us to write the event into existence through the image, is the site in which these "hearts and souls" are won and lost.[14] And it is in

---

[11] The failure of the cinema (the Kino that saw for us) was that it brought the image to us: it literally saw for us. In effect, Kino took the place of God but man wanted a God that was in his image (and not the other way); television fulfills this function as it does not see for you – television brings you there where you can see for yourself through (and perhaps more aptly, in) television.

[12] Mike Deaver, deputy chief of staff during Reagan's first term famously said, "In the competition between the ear and the eye, the eye always wins."

The quotation from Deaver is take from Glenn Elert. (1992). "Television and the Presidency: How the News Affects Our Perceptions" which can be found at http://hypertextbook.com/eworld/president.shtml

[13] This anecdote was shared with me via email communication with Andrew Feenberg. (4 November, 2003).

[14] The exception of course is when you are at the event itself. This is the only situation of an authentic event: one in which occurs in a particular time and space: in this case, you are very much a part of the event itself. In any other case, it is television that allows one to create an event (from that event) – one that is as real as the event itself (in fact they are no longer distinguishable).

For instance, in the case of the Iraqi people, they are very much a part of the event that we have called the Gulf War (whether events have names or not, or is there a possibility of naming an event, is another question that has to be examined elsewhere). The interesting thing to consider is that for an Iraqi that lives in Basra, (s)he is very much part of the event in Basra, but her/ his perception of 'events' in Baghdad are still very much formed via being a spectator in television. In this instance, there is a duality that is taking place – a duality that is indifferentiable. In fact, one might go as far as saying that the moment

this very regard that Bush Sr. has been more successful than the Jr. version: the management (it is selection and more importantly what is left out that is so crucial here) of images was far more skillfully handled the first time round.[15]

***

Is this hangover of presence – this inability to cope sans the privileging of sight – the revenge of God for his death?

God the All-Seeing: who is also the same God that attempted to keep this gift of seeing from humankind. Prometheus was punished by Zeus for the gift of fire – the gift that was reserved for the Gods; for in some sense, with fire, there is no more darkness and humankind would have been able to see all the time. A similar punishment was dealt to Lucifer for he was literally the Bringer of Light to humankind: eat from the tree and "you will be like gods knowing good and evil."[16] Both Prometheus and Lucifer were banished for literally attempting to en-lighten humankind – their gift to humankind was the gift of questioning what God says (in the form of the law of Zeus, and of the command to not eat from a particular tree: "did God really tell you not to eat fruit from any of the trees in the garden?"[17])

In some sense, humankind has accepted the gift of both Prometheus and Zeus: humankind rebelled against God by creating idols. And in doing so, humankind simulated God, causing God to disappear into and within the images themselves. In fact, the image of God over-takes and becomes more important than God: this is the murder of God that is attempted. For how else can all religions pass decrees in the name of God (which in effect is a claim to having knowledge of God – who is completely and utterly un-knowable – if they have not killed God; or at least made Her/ Him disappear). Even Islam (who tries to hide this fact by banning representations of *Allah*) has succumbed to this temptation: for sans this murder, how can the place of the Ayatollah (or any Imam – for the position of Ayatollah is merely a public perception of the greatness of any particular Imam to begin with) hold. By claiming to be the executor of the will of *Allah*, who is the legislator and judiciary of everything on earth, in effect, and the only way that that can occur, is if the Ayatollah deems himself the person who knows *Allah's* will: in order to execute Allah's 'will', what the Ayatollah has to first do is execute *Allah*.[18]

(s)he begins to attempt to 'understand' the event that (s)he is part of in Basra – without taking into account an element of un-understandability that is always already part of any event, or even any act of interpretation – her perception of it is in the realm of news already.

[15] This is especially true when you consider that the "hearts and minds" of the people were won in 1990 on a false premise as well: all credit for the tale of baby massacres goes to Hill & Knowlton here. What the first Bush administration managed to ensure was that far less competing images emerged (who cares about testimonials of soldiers that were actually there): in this manner, Bush Sr. managed to monopolized the Oracle.

In playing the priestess of the Oracle, one no longer monopolizes the Word, and what is heard, but rather what is seen: the Image is the key now.

[16] Genesis 3:4

[17] Genesis 3:1

[18] Perhaps it is the Sufis, with their insistence that *Allah* can never be known, that escape this temptation to murder Allah. For all action is made in the fidelity to *Allah* – and not in the claim that it is done in *Allah's* name.

But the death of God is the very revenge of God for the rebellion of humankind. For it is not that humankind has succeeded in killing God (only the vanity of humankind would allow us to entertain the possibility of killing God) – God's disappearance into and within the Image is because (S)he realizes that (S)he is no longer needed: the All-Seeing image has already been internalized by humankind.

This is exactly the same logic that is at play when the British granted independence to Malaya (especially Singapore, which was always the most important colony of the British Occupation of South East Asia). Independence was granted not so much to grant freedom to the people in Singapore, but only because the British realized that colonization was complete: there is no country in the world that is more obsessed with speaking Queen's English than Singapore; not even the Queen herself.

***

> Television showed precisely a tele-vision, that is a vision that is no longer the possibility of seeing what is at hand, and if it taught us anything, it was this: What fascinates us robs us of our power to give sense; drawing back from the world at the moment of contact, it draws us along, fascinated, blinded, exploded.[19]

This is the indeterminability and indistinctability of television – it brings us closer to, but at the same time further from, the event than ever before – for it is no longer an event that we are talking about (as far as this is even possible) anymore, but a 'media event.' And it is this media event – this mediated event – that appears clear, distilled and understandable, transparent. The transparency that draws us into itself – seduces us – by being completely and utterly meaningless, "emptied of any signified; it is a site of evacuation, the hemorrhaging of meaning."[20]

At this point of meaninglessness, it is also trans-meaning: this is precisely the point in which no meaning is possible and all meaning is possible: the point where "the idea that the actual person is the author of the letter forms a natural and easy transition to the actuality."[21]

Where the writer is not writing any longer, but is written.

It is this absence of meaning – this void – that allows us to write meaning into existence; it is this void that sutures us. In effect, television sets the scene for the perfect crime – the murder of reality; the emptying of the signified, literally the "dead letter" which can then be impregnated (make no mistake; we are in the realm of necrophilia). For like the "great stars or seductresses [who] never dazzle because of their talent or intelligence, but because of their absence,"[22] it is this absence of meaning that allows us, and not only allows but drives us to the rituals of

---

[19] Avital Ronell. (1998). "Trauma TV" in *Finitude's Score: Essays for the End of the Millennium.* pp.317.

[20] Ibid. pp.311.

[21] Soren Kierkegaard. (1997). *The Seducer's Diary.* pp.159.

[22] Jean Baudrillard. (1990). *Seduction.* pp.96.

necromancy, from which meaning "rises from the ashes, like the phoenix, or from their mirror, like the seductress."[23]

> There is no God behind the images, and the very nothingness they conceal must remain a secret. The seduction, fascination and "aesthetic" attraction of all the great imaginary processes lies here: in the effacing of every instance, be it the face and every substance, be it desire – in the artificial perfection of the sign.[24]

It is the not so much the "nothingness" that must "remain a secret" for if there was nothing to conceal, then a revelation of nothingness still remains nothing. But rather it is the fact that a secret always already contains nothing. It is precisely this revelation – a revelation that absolutely nothing is revealed – that must be concealed, for this is the secret of appearances, the secret of Death. The secret "that death itself shines by its absence, that death can be turned into a brilliant and superficial appearance, that it is itself a seductive surface ..."[25]

***

> The disciple of a Sufi of Baghdad was sitting in an inn one day when he heard two figures talking. He realized that one of them was the Angel of Death. "I have several calls to make in this city," said the Angel to his companion. The terrified disciple concealed himself until the two had left. To escape Death, he hired the fastest horse he could, and rode day and night to the far distant desert city of Samarkand. Meanwhile, Death met the disciple's teacher, and they talked of this and that. "And where is your disciple, so-and-so?" asked Death. "I suppose he is at home, where he should be, studying," said the Sufi. "That is surprising," said Death, "for here he is on my list. And I have to collect him tomorrow, in Samarkand, of all places."[26]

The careless whisper of Death. A pure sign, devoid of any meaning – certainly not for the disciple. Just a passing statement. Indeed imbued with some form of meaning by the disciple, but devoid from the sign itself, with absolutely nothing to do with the sign. Only the ghost of the sign. But it is the empty sign that is so enticing; full of un-intentional appeal, for even Death knew nothing of it. This is seduction.

***

But the troubling question remains, now stronger than ever before – if we impregnate as we desire, how is it that we impregnate terror into the void that is the "dead letter" (of news)? How is the 'media event' that has become the event, superceded the event – or at least has hidden the event within the image (the media

---

[23] Ibid. pp.96.

[24] Ibid. pp.94.

[25] Ibid. pp.97

[26] This is a famous version of an Islamic parable "Death in Samarkand" that is found at http://home.tiscali.be/jan.kersschot/whodies.htm. This version can also be found in *Think – A compelling introduction to Philosophy.* (1999). Oxford: Oxford University Press. pp.110-111.

27

is the cause of the disappearance of the event) – the realm in which terror is narrated into existence, the very terror which terrorizes ourselves?

The scene for the perfect crime – the murder of reality – has been set. But thankfully (or perhaps not so), no crime is perfect; even though the reality that we create is more real than the Real, the ghost of the Real remains to haunt us. Not by resurrecting itself, but by allowing itself to die. For like God, the Real has allowed its own murder (by virtue of its disappearance) because it has realized that it has already won.

If the crime is not perfect, then someone has to be caught – this is the only way in which the law legitimizes itself (in this sense, a perfect crime would have to be crime-less). But herein lies the problem: where do we begin to hunt for this criminal; this elusive slipping figure that we can never seem to find?

This is the truth (and the eternal failing) of the mirror: one can never see oneself. Which is why, the arrest can never be made.[27]

Shiny-shiny, shiny boots of leather. Whiplash girl-child in the dark.[28]

We write terror into existence. And in doing so, we create the situation in which we are governed (perhaps 'ruled' is more apt; a rule by the situation that we have created ourselves: a rule by self-governance is taking place here) with greater and greater intensity. In essence, we are not only chaining ourselves and pulling the chord ever tighter: we have also designed this very chord ourselves and commissioned the tying with utmost precision.

"You have forgotten something," she whispered naughtily, "the most important thing."

"A condition?"

"Yes, that I should always appear in my furs," she exclaimed. "but I promise you that I shall, if only because it makes me feel like a despot. I want to be very cruel with you, do you understand?"

"Shall I sign the contract?" I asked.

"Not yet," said Wanda, "I shall first add the conditions and then you can sign in all due form."[29]

---

[27] This assumes that arrest is desired. But of course arrest is desired – for the fantasy is one of complete freedom. But the fantasy can and must never be fulfilled – that is where the arrest comes into play: we desire the freedom but intrinsically woven into this desire (let's call it that for a moment) is what will never allow this freedom to be complete; which is why we will continue and always continue to arrest it; for it is the fulfillment of this freedom that will unleash the absolute horrors of the Real: this is the function of terror itself – written into freedom in order that freedom itself is never completely set free.

[28] Lou Reed. (1966). *Venus in Furs.*

[29] Leopold von Sacher-Masoch. (1971). *Venus in Furs.* pp.53-54.

Severin has his furs. But this is not the key aspect for it matters little what the exact fetish is. It is Wanda who reveals the key to the fantasy; the fantasy lies in signing in "due form." For it is through formalized rituals that the masochist achieves her/his jouissance. The fantasy is brought into play (it is play that is crucial here – it is a game, with all its accompanying rules) through this contract with the Other. The question to be asked then is not 'what "furs" are we desiring', but rather the manner in which this desire takes shape: 'shape' is the exact term to be used here, for it is the form of the desire that is crucial and not its manifestation.[30]

But in order to venture into the realm of the negotiated contract, we have to examine the parties involved: Severin and Wanda: I and the Other.

***

> "My" – what does this word designate? Not what belongs to me, but what I belong to, what contains my whole being, which is mine insofar as I belong to it.[31]

My. The self. And this indistinction that lies with(in) the Self (and the Other). Which opens the question of, is the Other wholly Other, or is the Other part of the Self (whilst perhaps maintaining its Otherness)? It is this indistinction that lies in the Other, and results in its being "mine insofar as I belong to it"; in this sense, the Other is (n)either mine (n)or ever Wholly Other.

It is in this light that we can see that the common usage of a contract being 'between' two parties is more accurate than usually regarded. For the contract is not the binding of both parties in the sense of a collapsing into, a becoming one, but rather the coming together in the acknowledgment of the impossibility of this joining. Which is why the final statement in the marriage vow is "what God unites, man must not divide": if the two parties truly became one, the vow would have read, 'man cannot divide.' The fact that it reads "must not divide" is the implicit acknowledgement that there is no unity that occurs; it is an attempted unity – for if there was true unity, then it could not be divided; it this case, there is at best an unstable one that can be divided by man, but "must not" be. Even in marriage, man cannot undo the action of Zeus: the Androgyn remains split forever.

But to deny that a 'uniting' takes place is probably untrue as well: it is the determination (as far as that is even possible) of this 'uniting' that must be considered. Perhaps this is the moment of the resurrection of the Androgyn – but not the same being in its original state; that has forever been divided by Zeus. Instead, it is the memory of this being that brings the two together – in this sense, the 'uniting' is one of a fidelity to the Androgyn rather than the actual original (whatever that even begins to mean) being itself. In this sense, the new Androgyn that is formed in this unity is another Androgyn, a different Androgyn, a return of the same that is always already slightly different, a third that is always already new.

---

[30] To assert that the content of a contract completely does not matter is probably not true. But the fact remains that the only reason why the contract binds you, is that it appeals to a network – the Law, the community, the socius etc. Sans this network (which is used in the Latourian sense), the contract would cease to have any power whatsoever. In this sense, it is the form of the contract – the ritual of the contract – that first takes hold of you. In exactly what manner it binds you lies in the details, that is, the content.

[31] Soren Kierkegaard. (1997). *The Seducer's Diary*. pp. 146.

This is what Walter Benjamin meant when he said that we can only remember the future: the 'uniting' of the two into the new (the third which is always already unknowable, at least from the present, and hence must be a unity that occurs in fidelity to a future possibility): which is also why hope always lies in the past (through fidelity to Androgyn, and also to the possibilities that were never actualized, such as the possibility of the Androgyn being two parts as – as opposed to 'in' - one).

The new Androgyn: not a fusing of man and woman into one, but rather a indistinct being which is (n)either man (n)or woman.

Which then brings us to the only truly authentic statement that can be made: when asked what this 'third' is, the only true thing that one can say is that "I don't know," the utterance that truly terrifies us, and makes us tremble (which should be a hint of the mystery that lies with(in) it). For what this utterance reveals is not so much a lack of knowledge about a particular realm (in the sense of 'I don't know what 2 and 2 amounts to') but rather a more profound "I don't know what 'I' even begins to mean." It is at the point of this utterance, this complete and utter un-knowingness, that we glimpse death – the Absolute Unknown – which is also the Absolute Other. For it is only in grasping (which is impossible, so glimpsing will have to suffice for the moment), this Absolute Other, and this absolute incomprehensibility, that one catches a glimpse of what is 'my', and what is the 'I'.

It is in this zone of indistinction between the 'I' and the 'Other' that the contract is signed: in this sense, the question can never be who the contract is signed 'by' but rather who the contract was signed 'between.' For at the point of signing, the contract was signed between 'I', a simulated Other, and the 'Absolute Other': in fact, the only distinct member of this triumvirate is the simulated Other by virtue of the fact that the 'I' and the 'Absolute Other' are both (n)either mine (n)or wholly Other and completely unknowable respectively. The simulated Other – the simulacra as Lucretius describes – is the zone in which the contract (and any form of communication for that matter) takes place.

This is the very zone where the jouissance of the masochist is located: neither in the pain nor pleasure that is physically felt by the masochist (nor his 'mistress'/ 'master') but in the creation of the contract itself. The jouissance is found in this simulated Other that is always already absent – the lack, the gap, that allows the fantasy to continue endlessly, but never completely fulfill itself – is the very thing that Wanda notes, when she whispered naughtily, "you have forgotten something …. The most important thing." "A condition?" [Severin]. "Yes …"[32]

Wanda, Wanda, where are you Wanda?

The social contract is what binds us. For one, we are never the ones who decide what is in this 'contract' to begin with: this opens the question as to how much of a contract is this then? How much of this contract is negotiated then? What this does not negate is the fact that this is the very contract in which we are obliged to live by.

---

[32] Leopold von Sacher-Masoch. (1971). *Venus in Furs.* pp.53-54. [this new sequence is mine]

This then opens the question of whether this social contract is a sadistic contract, in the sense of one that effaces your will.[33] When one is subjected to the social contract, which manifests in the Law of the state, the question of one's will is moot, which is why when the Law is concerned, the contestation lies in the realm not of whether something is fair or not (for this takes into regard the will of the person), but rather whether one has followed or not: it is always only a question of obedience.[34] But each and every time one votes in an election, are we not in some way voting for that very contract as well? This is the masochistic element; the election process of every state is masochism at play: a negotiation with the state under which contract (and in certain states, a more direct selection of a particular 'Wanda' for a specific period of time) we are bound to. Perhaps this is the only instance in which one can revive the term Sado-Masochistic again: a masochistic negotiation (through the elections) which will enter us into a sadistic agreement (when our wills are effaced by the social contract). The state is the realm in which S&M lies.

The moment we select, we have effectively signed the contract. In effect, we always already sign ourselves away to a contract that effaces our will: we sign ourselves into a state of exception[35] as the "sovereign is, at the same time, inside and outside the juridical order."[36] In essence, we have always already signed ourselves via a masochistic agreement into a relationship sans any safe-word.

***

> slave screams he spends his life learning conformity
> slave screams he claims he has his own identity
> slave screams he's going to cause the system to fall
> slave screams but he's glad to be chained to that wall[37]

It is this fantasy of, and for, freedom that sets the scene (it is always a formal, ritualized scene) for the creation of the Other not in, but with the state (this is the third that we were speaking of; the simulated Other). But if this is a scene of the jouissance of the Subject, then why is the slave screaming? Should (s)he not be in the throes of joys when "chained to that wall"?

One must never forget that it is fantasy itself that must never be fulfilled. And it is terror that fulfils this function for the Subject. In effect, terror fulfils a dual function – in reading and (re)writing terror into existence, terror both allows the

---

[33] This was a thought raised during a conversation with Kenny Png. (29 October, 2005): Singapore.

[34] Consider a contention in a trial between murder and manslaughter: even when the Law is considering the 'intent' of the accused, it is not 'intent' that resides in the realm of Will, that is, the internal considerations of the person. The Law can only judge a person on the signs displayed by the accused/ defendant; in this sense, the Will of the person (which can never actually be known) must be put aside.

[35] Agamben argues that the 'concentration camp' is the model of the modern state; that is, it is not an exception in a state. The state of exception is the norm now – the state is the concentration camp.

This argument can be found amongst other places at Giorgio Agamben. (1998). *Homo Sacer: Sovereign Power and Bare Life.*

[36] Ibid. pp.1.

[37] Trent Reznor. (1992). "Happiness is Slavery" in *Broken E.P.*

creation of the Other in order that we are "chained to that wall" whilst at the same time ensuring that the wall is never completed (terror as the singularity that does not allow globalization to complete its own logic). In our fantasy of, and for, freedom, terror ensures that the state denies us this freedom that we crave, and at the same time, ensures us just enough freedom (both at the moment of choice, and as the incompleteness of this slavery): in effect, the gladness[38] of the slave occurs in that indistinct moment of being (n)either free (n)or in servitude (or at least being in servitude to a master of her/ his own creation).

And just like "in sadism no less than in masochism, there is no direct relation to pain"[39]: terror should be regarded as an effect only.

---

[38] In some way, being able to scream is the moment of jouissance itself for it is the moment in which the Subject enacts its own singularity, its own self, whilst being bound, being completely selfless: this is precisely the gap – between self and otherness – that allows for jouissance.

[39] Gilles Deleuze. (1999). *Coldness and Cruelty.* pp.121.

The Gift

When Samson pushed apart the columns, pulling the house of the Philistines down upon himself, there was an originary gift – the gift of his life. For at the very moment that he brought down the columns, he had offered himself up as a gift. The Philistines that had captured him and bound him to their pillars reciprocated with their lives.[1]

> Then Samson prayed, "Sovereign Lord, please remember me; please God, give me my strength one time more, so that with this one blow I can get even with the Philistines for putting out my two eyes." So Samson took hold of the two middle columns holding up the building. Putting one hand on each column, he pushed against them and shouted, "Let me die with the Philistines!"[2]

Samson offered himself in a symbolic exchange. In his final plea, he cried to God to give him strength one last time: "let me die with the Philistines." In offering his life, Samson forces reciprocation from the Philistines – after all this is the economy that we are working in: every action demands reciprocation (let alone a surplus value). When Samson offered up his life, the Philistines had no choice but to reciprocate with their own lives. And thus "Samson killed more people at his death than he had killed during his life."[3] Perhaps a more precise line should have been: Samson killed more people because of his death. For in offering himself up, he had given the Philistines no recourse. For in life, when attacking them, they had a right, almost an obligation, to defend themselves. It is this same obligation – the obligation of reciprocity – that Samson appeals to in sacrificing himself.

This is the economy that every suicide bomber appeals to. It is the logic of reciprocity that governs the socius; and it is this very logic that is the spectre that haunts us.

But in order to examine this logic, we would have to take a closer look at what constitutes this symbolic economy. For Samson does not engage in a direct exchange with the Philistines – his plea for strength was to God; and as such, his intent to kill the Philistines was also mediated through (and by) God. In this sense, at this very moment, Samson had no real idea whether he had the strength to carry out the feat he intended or not. Should God have not acceded to his pleas, Samson would have been left standing in the middle of the room with his hands on the columns and nothing more; perhaps the Philistines would have construed this as part of the entertainment that he was brought there to perform in the first place (which is assuming they had a good sense of humour: the higher likelihood is they would have killed him for attempting to kill 5 Kings of the Philistines). So at the very moment of the appeal, this moment of indistinction, what Samson was doing was offering himself, through the gift of his life, as a sacrifice to God in order that he is granted the strength. In fact the only guarantee that Samson had was his death – if God had granted him the strength he pleaded for, the roof would have collapsed on him as well, and if God rejected his plea, the Philistines would have executed him. In this

---

[1] The tale of Samson is taken from the Judges 13-17.

[2] Judges 16:28-30

[3] Ibid.

manner, it was only the gift of his life, the gift of his death, that was offered up to God. And only when this was granted, did the deaths of the Philistines come about. In this sense, the death of the Philistines was the symbolic exchange that was taking place – there was no real exchange between Samson and the Philistines. It was a pure gift of Samson to God; the result of this was that God reintroduced the concept of economy into it – and as such turned a an-economic gift and re-inscribed it into the economy of reciprocity – and the result of that was the death of the Philistines.

In this very same way, there is always an uncertainty at the point in which a suicide bomber straps on the bombs around her/ him self, for there is absolutely no way of knowing the outcome of the attempt. What the suicide bomber is doing is offering her/ him self up as a pure gift – a gift that is only present in the act of giving itself – to either a transcendental being (by way of a God) or to a cause (which really is a transcendental being in another manifestation). What is offered is the life of the bomber her/ him self – in this case, it does not matter if there is a group of suicide bombers; each individual offers her/ him self as an absolute singularity here. This life is offered as a sacrifice – the gift of life, which is also at the same time the gift of death (for what is a sacrifice but the offering of the only gift one can offer, the gift of one's life, one's death).

The Gift and giving: giving the Gift

The gift. And not a gift. A true gift is always already the gift and never merely a gift. For when one says 'a gift' it refers to a gift being one in a line of gifts. But in the case of 'the gift,' it remains – here 'becomes' might be a better word, but mayhaps we should allow for this indeterminacy – a singularity.

In that singularity, the gift is completely irreplaceable – in this sense, it must be completely in-exchangeable. Hence there can be no value – or at least value as is commonly known, in the sense of exchange value (or if we want to be more radical, is any valuation really outside the system of exchange) – attributed to the gift. It must be valueless and invaluable – completely devoid of value and beyond value at the same time.

The gift is (n)either valueless (n)or invaluable.

Which means – considering that this can still mean anything – that the gift, in its complete indeterminacy (if indeterminacy can be complete: perhaps its completeness is one which allows for an incompleteness within its very structure of completeness), must then take place within a structure that does not allow for exchange to occur. In this way, it operates in a an-economic structure: a singular gift, completely irreplaceable, un-exchangeable and irreducible. What this suggests is that the gift is also completely devoid of any reciprocity. The gift is just given – in some sense the gift is in the act of giving itself. For only sans object can anything be truly devoid of reciprocity. Which then makes the gift an object-less giving; the act itself is all, the act itself is everything: the gift must always already be devoid of itself (in the precise sense of lacking an object).

The gift exists in the realm of an impossible exchange. And it is this impossibility that guarantees its singularity. It is also this impossibility that haunts us. Which is why the suicide bomber is such an enigma in modern society – we no longer have any understanding of singularities. Capitalism has propelled us towards complete flatness – how else can total and complete exchange take place; everything exists on the same scale. The saying "every man (and by this extension woman) has a price" has to be taken with the utmost seriousness, and in a completely literal sense. It is by no means metaphorical. In fact, in the world we live in, metaphors are dead: George Orwell pre-empted this when he coined the term "dying metaphors."[4] It is the singularity of the suicide bomber – this figure that escapes interpretation – an enigma in the truest sense – a black hole that sucks everything else into it that leaves us trembling.[5]

The lack of an object does not mean that the gift is devoid of any meaning though. On the contrary, it opens up the complete possibilities of meaning(s) for the gift. For once given, the gift is opened to the complete and utter act of reception – just because it is un-reciprocable does not mean that it cannot be received. The reception of the gift is what allows for the act of giving – and hence the gift itself – to occur. And sans object, the gift then becomes completely open to all interpretation. And it is this attempt to conceive (the interpretation is the conception of the object that previously is devoid in the gift) that forces the gift back into the realm of the economy: it moves it from a an-economic back into an economic system: it moves it from 'the' gift back into 'a' gift.

Consider the tale of the (attempted) sacrifice of Isaac.[6] When Abraham brought Isaac up to Mount Moriah as a sacrifice to the Lord, he was asked by Isaac, "... where is the lamb for the sacrifice?" To which his answer was: "God himself will provide one." At the moment in which he raised his knife to sacrifice Isaac, Abraham has already killed him – this is the gift that God required from him. It was an objectless sacrifice – the act of killing Isaac was the sacrifice itself. Unknown to Abraham at the time, his response (if one can call it a response at all for it was an empty statement; it was neither a truth nor a lie to Isaac),[7] was precisely what

---

[4] It is capitalism (and its need for complete and utter exchange) that necessarily sucks language into its logic. In this manner, all metaphors are pointless – language must function; and in order to guarantee maximum performativity (Lyotard), all words must have repeatability. For that to occur, all metaphors (if we can still call them that) must be dead. In this manner, there is no more new image to evoke, and all words merely become currency stored in a data base of 'language' to be used.

For Orwell's full article, refer to George Orwell. (1946). "Politics and the English Language."

[5] For something is only a secret, a mystery, if it leaves us trembling. This is the full sense of the *mysterium tremendum* that Jacques Derrida speaks of: a secret that cannot be shared or even spoken of. For a true secret is in the unknowing – the secret is in the secret itself: you and I share a secret only if we both do not know what this secret is – it is sans object, it is beyond knowing. And it is this that gives the secret its great power, a power that causes us to tremble before it.

The Wizard only makes Dorothy and friends tremble when they do not look beneath the mask. The moral of the tale lies not so much in that the un-masking (or de-mystifying) of a secret is what frees one from the fear. The true moral of the *Wizard of Oz* is that a secret can never be unveiled. Even after looking behind the curtain, there is no explanation as to why the fear existed in the first place. The man behind the curtain is merely an operator of the machine. But the Wizard remains completely and utterly unknown. This is the true enigma of the tale – the secret of the Wizard (who always will remain a secret) is what makes Dorothy and friends tremble.

For a discussion of the *mysterium tremendum* please refer to Jacques Derrida. (1995.) *The Gift of Death*. (esp. pages 1-35).

[6] Genesis 22:1-19

[7] Slavoj Zizek might call Abraham's strategy one of the pervert in the very sense that he uses truth to tell a lie. For his very words "God will provide one" is true (despite that fact that he doesn't quite know it at that very instance), but he uses it to cover up the lie (which is that he is going to kill his son).

occurred; it was God who provided the object for the holocaust – the ram that was burnt in Isaac's place. To be very precise though, it cannot be said that the ram died for Isaac, for no one can die in your place: death is an absolute singularity that one must undertake for oneself. A true gift – the gift – must always already involve death; in some sense, death is the only gift. So perhaps we should say then that the ram was burnt instead of Isaac.[8]

But one must never forget that it was God who provided the object for the holocaust. In this very manner, it is the recipient of the gift who conceives of the object and not the giver. The giver just gives. The receiver must receive (there is no element of choice in this) – the role of the receiver is not in the choosing to receive or not to receive the gift, but rather in the creation of the object of the gift itself.[9]

The (gift-less) Gift

At the point of giving, the gift is a pure gift – there is nothing but the giving itself (and the symbolic – and very real act – of the giving of the life, the death, of the suicide bomber); there is no object. Which suggests that at the point of giving, there is no-thing that can be ascribed to the act of giving, the gift itself, sans object, sans signifier: strictly speaking, no signified can be attached to the act; it is an act without any possibility of signification that has taken place.

But it is at this point that we choose to play God.

For the receiver of the suicide bomber, and the bombings, which is whom the gift is offered to (whether you are the willing recipient of not is never the question) inscribes the gift back into the economy. In fact, the receiver is the one who produces the signifier and then the signified – this is what re-inscribes the gift into the game of communication; the game of signs; the orgasmic ecstasy of communication.[10]

This only occurs not despite an act without signification, nor even in-spite, but rather because the suicide bomber has offered a pure gift to the receiver. And this pure gift is what draws the receiver into her/ him self: in the impossible exchange that the receiver is faced with, the receiver reacts with her/ his own self (it does not

---

[8] Much of this reading of the tale of Abraham and Isaac is inspired by Derrida's interpretation. This can be found in full at Jacques Derrida. (1995). *The Gift of Death*.

[9] Which is why a gift cannot be considered a neutral thing. In some sense, there is always a sadistic element to the gift – it is given and the receiver has absolutely no choice in whether they want to accept or not. The gift is imposed upon them. There is no contract (as in the case of the masochist where the master and the slave come to a precise contractual agreement on what is to be done and what is not to be done). The gift is put onto the receiver – sans consideration of the receiver at all.

[10] Communication for the sake of communication itself: where there is nothing to the act of communication but the act itself. This is the ecstasy of communication.

Jean Baudrillard. (1988). *The Ecstasy of Communication*.

And or course, in the orgasm there is always already the hint of death, a momentary death – a small death that occurs. Which is in no way a nihilistic moment – there is no fatalism in this momentary death but the very opposite that occurs. A celebration (and recalling – for one can only recall the future) of death – which can only occur in a out-pouring of life itself.

matter if the exchange is occurring on two separate realms – all exchange is simulated to begin with; in this sense, they have always already been occurring on separate realms).

It is the impossibility of this exchange that seduces us, draws us into itself; its indistinction being the lure that pulls us, and it is our very resistance, a resistance to the idea that this exchange is impossible; it is our complete belief – nay faith is the precise term here (blindness a very crucial aspect in it) – in the possibility of communication (in the form of sign systems, and reciprocity, even if we conceive of it as an utopian concept) that allows the empty sign to seduce us. It is this play with possibility – the empty sign never remains empty, it is the sign that is always already awaiting impregnation – which seduces the receiver into inseminating the empty sign.

The gift is seductive.

[It is not a strategy of seduction for that would imply that there was a motive behind the gift – it is capitalism that has to see it as a strategy for without an aim, there can be no outcome, or more aptly, no calculable outcome – and hence no possibility of reproducing it.]

This is the reason why the suicide bomber trans-fixes us, and captures our entire being in and within her/ him self. For we have lost all comprehension of the seductive already (just recall how many time have you been chastised for being unproductive; which really just translates to 'what you are doing has no reproducible meaning'). It is this very meaninglessness of the act of giving that has captured us, its alien-ness that transfixes us, sucking us into itself.

And our only desperate defence (if we can even call it that) is to violently shove it back into the realm of the economy.

To our own death.

Motives (motifs) and motivations

To speak of motives is to speak of an exchange, an aim and then a result – a measurable result to be exact. In this manner one can calculate the success (and failure; for what is success without the inclusion of failure).[11] More crucially, with the calculability comes reproducibility: this is the logic that capitalism functions on, and cannot function without.

In this sense, perhaps motives can be spoken of when one is considering the organization which is behind the suicide bomber – when one speaks of why a certain organization sends persons on particular missions, an aim, a motive and a result can then be brought into the equation (and make no mistake, it is indeed an equation that we speak of in such instances). In fact, most discourse on terrorism (and even on suicide bombings) revolve around such topics – but what else do we expect; the

---

[11] No 'motivational speaker' can function without this concept – despite all their claims that one must focus on success, failure is the hinge of the entire discourse. It is the demonizing of failure that all 'motivational speakers' focus on – what religions do with the Devil, the motivational speaker does with failure. (Billy Graham would probably be a motivational-religious, as much as that is tautological, speaker).

discourse of capitalism must revolve around capital (a discourse that does not involve equations, or more precisely equitabilities, will not be tolerated).

But that does not even begin to look at the singularity that is the suicide bomber. A discourse that revolves around motives is an attempt to drag the suicide bomber – the singularity that does not conform to equitabilities, that does not allow for calculability – back into the realm of exchangeability.

This is the revenge of capital on terror; removing its singular weapon and trans-figuring it into merely another unit of exchange, a currency that is flat.

Perhaps then all we can speak of is motifs.

There is undeniably a ritual involved. One of the better known manifestations of the modern suicide bomber is the *Kamikaze* pilot, the bringer of the Divine Wind. Much of the Western analysis (and criticism) revolves around the fact that before flying, the pilots were pumped full of amphetamines in order to allow them to fly their planes into targets – to transform themselves into weapons. But this argument misses the entire point: their deaths do not occur at the point when their planes crash into the targets: their lives, and their death, were long already offered to the Emperor. On every mission the pilots follow the same ritual – a last meal together (Jesus seems to have made this fashionable, even state prisons have caught on), a last cigarette, a last cup of sake, and a bow to the Emperor. By the time the pilot is in the plane, he is already dead.

But regardless of the manifestations of the ritual, it is the offering of the gift of themselves sans guarantee that matters. For even in the case of the *Kamikaze* bomber, the only assurance that he has is his death. And that is his gift.

This opens the question of martyrdom and the *Houri*: in the case of the Islamic suicide bomber, many have claimed that their motivation the chance to achieve the status of a martyr and receive 72 *fair women of Paradise* as their reward. But is not the definition of martyrdom left to *Allah* (who's Will can never be known – even the writings of prophets and holy men are called interpretations, which is completely different from knowing). In this sense, it is only the life of the suicide bomber that is offered up to *Allah* (in the hope perhaps – but hope is a completely difference structure from an offer of exchange; there is no reciprocity in hope); there is nothing more than a an-economic gift there. It can be argued that the bombers have been persuaded by the clerics that *Allah's* Will is such, but even if you take that into consideration, it does not negate the fact that the suicide bomber walks her/ his path alone for no one can die another's death; only you can die for yourself, only you can offer your own death.[12] In this sense, the instance of the gift – for in the case of death, and the gift, it always occurs at the precise instance of giving – occurs at the very moment it is offered, the moment when the suicide bomber straps on the

---

[12] The Japanese ritual suicide, *Seppuku*, is interesting in this respect: in order to complete the act, the person committing *Seppuku* requires another to decapitate her/ him. This raises the question of whether it takes a member of the socius to allow your death to occur – or whether one's death can occur on one's own. However, even in *Seppuku*, the death of the person happens on their own – once the ritual begins, the person is already dead – all the other person is doing is finalizing the act itself; the symbolic structure of death is already complete. In this sense perhaps a member of the socius allows you to complete the act, but the symbolism of suicide is the singularity of the person's death that strikes out against socius' attempt to flatten individuality into a generality.

bombs. At this precise moment (s)he is already dead. The crucial aspect is that the death of the bomber occurs without any knowable response from *Allah* – and it is the very absence of the response that constitutes this as a pure gift.[13]

Is not hatred a motivation though? Perhaps it is – it is probably undeniable that the suicide bombers on September 11 2001 had a hatred for the United States of America (or probably more accurately what the US stood for). In-spite of this, it does not make their deaths any less an event – all deaths are singular – nor their suicides from being a gift at the instance of their deaths, or more precisely, the instance of the decisions of the deaths. The singularity of the suicide bomber is not completely separated from the economy that surrounds the act but it is a singularity that resides along with, and maybe even within the surrounding economy.[14]

But consider this as well: can we sacrifice something that we don't love? Is it even a sacrifice at all if we are merely giving away something that we don't want to begin with? It is this that makes the suicide bomber unique from any other suicide. Even as every death – independent of causes or motivations – is a singularity, there is a difference between the singularity of death as a gift of death, and the singularity of death as the ending of a life. For the gift only occurs in the case when the giving is done in love, and the giving is of love – despite the gift being object-less by definition, the giving occurs in a situation of love. The offering of Isaac is Abraham's gift to God because Isaac was the most beloved of Abraham. In the case of the suicide bomber, the gift is in the love (of her/ his life), and the love is in the gift – they are inseparable and indistinguishable.

It is the concept of love and sacrifice that leaves the West befuddled as they attempt to grapple with the perennial question of why a suicide bomber gives her/ his life when they had "so much to live for." In order to attempt to 'answer' this question, many resort to blaming Islamic clerics for their brain-washing, or to the 'Asian culture' of putting the society above the individual – all of which are nothing more than a desperate attempt to subsume the Other under a particular frame of thinking. Whilst there undoubtedly organizations that attempt to convince (or coerce) individuals into acts of violence (including suicide bombings), focusing on this completely misses the entire sacrificial aspect of the event: it is not that the suicide bomber kills her/ him self even though (s)he has "so much to live for" – it is

---

[13] This is the very question of faith itself. The structure of faith demands a lack of knowledge. For if one knows, it is no longer being faithful; it would have moved into the realm of fact. What is unique about faith is that one believes without knowing. But in the believing sans knowing, there is always already an element of doubt. And doubt is precisely the hinge that faith revolves around.

Which is why the crucial point of the story of Doubting Thomas does not lie in Jesus showing him his hands and side but rather in the statement, "Blessed are those who do not see and *yet* have believed" [my emphasis]: the key point of Jesus is in the "yet" – faith is believing whilst not having any particular reason to believe; it is a belief that exists in the un-believable: a belief that rests completely and totally on doubt.

And it is in this doubt; this moment of indiscernability, of whether *Allah* would treat the act as martyrdom or murder, that lies the gift.

[14] In this sense, the event is conceptualized very much like a Badiouian event. The subject does not exist in a separate world after the event – the new world is still a part of the existing world; it is a singularity that exists within and amidst generalities, amidst pluralities.

Alain Badiou. (2003). *Infinite Thought: truth and the return of philosophy.*

precisely because (s)he has so much to live for and is giving it up completely that it is a pure gift.

***

> [**4.157**] And their saying: Surely we have killed the Messiah, **Isa** son of Marium, the apostle of Allah; and they did not kill him nor did they crucify him, but it appeared to them so (like **Isa**) and most surely those who differ therein are only in a doubt about it; they have no knowledge respecting it, but only follow a conjecture, and they killed him not for sure.

Consider this: in Islam, it is not Jesus who dies on the cross. Perhaps this is a true understanding of the concept of sacrifice – that it requires no object. The divine nature in the man resides not in the death of flesh and blood, but rather in the very agreeing to die: in this sense, the passing of man into Divine was not on the cross but rather occurred in the garden of Gethsemane (even though this scene is not recorded in the *Quran*, the understanding of the Messianic moment remains): at the very moment when he answered "I am he," Jesus had sacrificed himself.

More interestingly, let us now consider the possibility that God demands a reciprocity for the sacrifice of his son – Jesus' sacrifice may be a true gift, but if God re-inscribed Samson's gift back into an economy, it is not inconceivable that God might do the same for Jesus' gift. In this manner, Christianity then forever suffers from this insufficiency: it is the only religion in which God does not allow humankind to save itself (the son of God dies for you; you are not even allowed to die for yourself).

What if suicide bombing is a reciprocation for God's gift to mankind? The only possible reciprocation for the act of love is death itself – the death of man – the giving up of her/ his life as a sacrifice to God. And this is captured in the suicide bomber. In some sense, when Islamic suicide bombers detonate themselves in Christian countries, they are fulfilling a duty that the Christians are unwilling to do: sacrifice their lives to reciprocate God's gift.

Crime of Passion

If the offering is carried out in love – or at least in fidelity to love[15] – what are we then to make of it? It seems problematic to completely withdraw the suicide bomber from the context – one cannot, and must never, forget that in the gift there is also the end result (even as it may be conceptually unconnected) of the deaths of people in the vicinity.

The question that reveals itself at this point is one which involves responsibility. In responding to God's call for a sacrifice, what happens to Abraham's

---

[15] Fidelity is taken here in the sense used by Alain Badiou, where even if there is no absolute (in this case 'love' or in another case 'truth'), the crucial element is the act is taken in a fidelity to this concept, even and perhaps even especially since it cannot (and must not even) be possible (to actualize; it is an impossibility to begin with). It is precisely this impossibility of actualizing 'love' that prevents it from being a totalizing concept; at the same time, its impossibility allows us to act 'as if' it was possible, in fidelity to its possibility.

responsibility to Isaac? For if every other is every other,[16] then a response to one is always already a privileging of one and a marginalization of the infinite other(s). At the very instant when Abraham "picked up his knife,"[17] he had decided to respond to God and abandon Isaac. There is no rationality to this decision: as Kierkegaard so aptly formulated, "the instant of decision is madness."[18]

Which suggests that at the moment when the suicide bomber presents her/ him self as the gift – imposes her/ him self as the gift – there is this mad choice, a choice beyond any cognition, any rationality, that is made, a choice that responds to an other (no doubt), but which also abandons all the other others: a choice sans reciprocity but also one that ends up sucking other(s) into its void (the moment the gift is re-inscribed – and it is always re-injected – into an economy of exchange).

The sacrifice always already carries along with it murder: the moment Abraham raised his knife, he not only already sacrificed Isaac, but also already murdered him. This is the zone of indistinction that the suicide bomber operates in: (s)he is always already responding to the other both as a gift of death, and a murderer.

***

One must never attempt to make the act clear, in the sense of attempting to fully and totally explaining (through analyzing) it, assuming that is even possible. For even if total comprehension is a utopian state, it is still is a fundamental axiom of most analysis. In doing so, in attempting to bring it to 'light', there is an attempt to make the event – the singular, which is ungraspable, or at least that which continues to elude grasping – transparent. This transparency is precisely the commodification of the event, the forcing of a singular into a system of exchange: when the singular becomes completely transparent, it is also completely representable. And through this representation, the event is encapsulated in a sign system, one that is completely and totally exchangeable: in effect, the event moves from a singular into a trans-event. This is the game of the capital, and one that we must refuse – this game of trans-mutation. For this would be the true crime.

***

In desperation we attempt to 'understand' the phenomenon of the suicide bomber. And in desperation we (try to) fit the suicide bomber into our schema of thought – a thought that is premised on performance; one that requires exchangeability (not to mention surplus value as both a product and a basis of that system itself). It is this thought – this re-introduction, this coercion – of the event of a suicide bombing into an economy (this refusal to accept a an-economical gift) that results in the need for reciprocation.[19]

---

[16] For an excellent analysis of the phrase "tout autre est tout autre", please refer to Jacques Derrida. (1996). "Tout Autre Est Tout Autre" in *The Gift of Death*. pp. 82-115.

[17] Genesis 22:10-11.

[18] Jacques Derrida. (1996). The Gift of Death. pp.65. which is probably a reference to Kierkegaard's *Philosophical Fragments*.

[19] The choice lies in the manner of reception, and acceptance. If you work within the economic paradigm, then obviously this symbolic gesture requires a return – and an escalation – otherwise the structure of surplus value would not be satisfied.

The reciprocation takes the form of death. For when there is a refusal to accept the gift, the only result can be a reciprocation of more death: 'more' is the only possible result – this is the surplus value that we speak of. This is the result that we see after the suicide bombings on September 11 2001: the wars in Afghanistan and Iraq.

Perhaps it is the incomprehensibility of the event that captures our imagination: the fact that no matter how much we attempt to 'analyze' this phenomena, and perhaps even the more we do so, it eludes our grasp, it continually slips away. This is why the phenomenon is an event: its incomprehensibility (and its complete voiding of interpretation, which by extension also makes it completely open to interpretation) and its utter indeterminacy.[20]

And it is this indeterminacy that makes the suicide bombing one of a gift-less gift. The gift of the suicide bomber is the gift of economy itself – the life of the suicide bomber, her/ his death, is her/ his gift; but at that very moment, the life, and death, that is given is also the very economy of exchange that is taking place, an economy that has no (possible) exchange. For there is no equivalent for the life that is offered (all talk of the number of casualties and the revenge that must follow suit in order to make them 'pay back' is obscene – and even more so to the casualties of the situation; in doing so one makes them merely a statistic). In the very event of suicide bombing, there is an impossible exchange that is taking place.

The gift of death is the gift of economy to itself. In the perfect and utter un-exchangeability of life, there is no gift in the gift; it is an objectless gift, it is a pure gift – a gift that resides only in the giving: a gift-less gift. A gift that gives giving, and can never be returned.

And it is this impossibility that has captured our imagination.[21]

---

[20] In some way, true understanding is one that accepts a lack of understanding, is "in want of understanding"; an acknowledgement of the plurality of this understanding, along with its in-completeness. It is this continual slippage of total understanding that acknowledges the madness that is part – and perhaps the hinge – of every decision.

For an analysis of the phrase "understanding is in want of understanding", please see Werner Hamacher. (1999). "Premises" in *Premises: Essays on Philosophy and Literature from Kant to Celan.*

[21] The previous three paragraphs were inspired by inter-personal conversation with Johannes Heide. (4 September 2005): Vienna.

The Arrest: Not 'stop or I'll shoot'; just go 'bang bang.'

> If you are dealing with a crowd with no central command, the tactical approach is to segment it into units, creating "clear zones," boundaries, and leaders. In fact, it is often necessary to organize a crowd by force in order to defeat it.[1]

The fear resides not in the fear of an inability to deal with a problem: the fear always lies in the inability to grasp the problem in the first place. For if the problem cannot be conceptualized, then there is no hope of solving it. Even the nature of 'solving' hints at the subsumption of the problem under the Subject's categories of 'understanding.'

This is the ghost of the Enlightenment which continues to haunt us: the belief in a transcendental truth that lies beneath all the layers: literally tearing the mask off in order that the Real is unveiled. Hence, the strategy has always been the 'understanding' of any issue through the thinking of it via categories: in effect, this is the assimilation and the subsumption of the problem into the categories pre-determined by the Subject – this is the violence of logic (which is then played out through language).[2] This is due to the need for synthesis to occur, which is the creation of surplus value.

We are horrified not when there are abnormalities, by way of oppositions, to our way of life; in this case, the reaction is always to either oppose and destroy it (which is the old logic of the state of Singapore with regard to homosexuality for instance: out-law it) or to subsume it under the dominant logic (which is the current strategy towards homosexuality: allow it under particular circumstances because of the 'pink dollar' that is generated). Capitalism is never concerned with morals and values, but operates under the logic of reproduction and surplus value: in this case, who cares who you sleep with, as long as you generate surplus. Surplus value is no longer limited to merely (re)producing another person; we have long ago already commodified persons (which means that they are exchangeable): can't produce another person, replace her/ him with something else. As long as there is (re)production everything is fine. This goes to explain why 'human resource' management is the new trend: we have come to realize that humans are resources (just manage their desires, and everything else falls into place). This is the very logic that is captured in the saying, "the happiest slave is one who thinks he is free."[3]

> Choose Life. Choose a job. Choose a career. Choose a family. Choose a fucking big television, choose washing machines, cars, compact disc players and electrical tin openers. Choose good health, low cholesterol, and dental insurance. Choose fixed interest mortgage repayments.

---

[1] As read in Finn Brunton. (2005). *Decontrol in Science, Music and War*. MA Thesis. Saas Fee: European Graduate School. pp. 56.

In this paragraph, Brunton is summarizing the riot-control strategies as elaborated upon by Rex Applegate.

[2] The violence that is done to multiplicities. For in the privileging of any one meaning, there is always already the marginalization of the infinite possibilities. The selection of any signified is the eradication of all the others.

[3] Constantly uttered by Kenny Png as a reaction to Trent Reznor's claim, "Happy the Slave."

Choose a starter home. Choose your friends. Choose leisurewear and matching luggage. Choose a three-piece suite on hire purchase in a range of fucking fabrics. Choose DIY and wondering who the fuck you are on a Sunday morning. Choose sitting on that couch watching mind-numbing, spirit-crushing game shows, stuffing fucking junk food into your mouth. Choose rotting away at the end of it all, pishing your last in a miserable home, nothing more than an embarrassment to the selfish, fucked up brats you spawned to replace yourself.

Choose your future.

Choose life.[4]

These are exactly the same choices presented to one at any shopping mall: choose between any shaving cream, it matters not for they are all exactly the same anyway. In effect, what we have is the simulation of choice that is taking place – choose by all means, make any decision as long as it does not have any real effects.[5]

In this sense, the crowd that is un-organized (which means that it cannot be subsumed under any existing logic) is a real threat: since it is un-calculable, the results (or effects if you prefer) cannot be pre-determined. The effects of the crowd will be un-determinable, new and real. It is for this precise reason that demonstrations of May 68 were so unique – their spontaneous origins. This is also why Lenin claims that all true revolutions need to happen on the spur of the moment; once organized and pre-planned, one can guarantee that the results can (and have) been pre-determined and hence will be subsumed by the existing logic, the incumbent hegemon.

"Elementary, my dear Watson"

The deduction of the law: the reduction of the law. In every attempt to solve a crime – even in the case of the perfect crime, when there is no crime, but just the signs of a crime – there is an attempt to reduce the problem (in the form of 'who did it') into a series of 'logical deductions'. In every instance of a trial in a court of law, the accused is judged according to the signs (no one except the very people that were at that time and space know what actually happened, and that is putting aside the consideration that they only know it from their own perspective) and judgment is passed according to these very signs. It is the swallowing of the event into a series of signs – this is the very reduction, the deduction, that is taking place.

---

[4] Andrew MacDonald. (Producer). & Danny Boyle. (Director). *Trainspotting*. (1996).

These were the opening lines in the movie, said by Mark Renton (played by Ewan McGregor). The screenplay was written by John Hodge and it was based on the novel of the same name by Irvine Welsh.

[5] Any real effect cannot be known a priori. Otherwise what we have are merely variations that have been anticipated; in effect the options in a simulated choice have already been pre-decided by the context. What this means is that the categories have determined the outcomes: whichever choice you make does not matter any longer (in effect they are always already the same choice): they are but alternatives.

This is the very function of 'human resource management': the management of desires is the giving of simulated choices – options – in order to satisfy the desire for choosing (for 'free will') but ensuring that no real choice will ever be made.

This is the role of the police.

For the function of the police is the arrest. And just like in a riot, "it is often necessary to organize a crowd by force in order to defeat it," stop it, arrest it. This is somewhat like what occurs when an analyst allows an analysand to believe that the cause of her/ his symptom has been found: it does not matter whether it is the true cause or not, as long as the symptoms cease, it is often good enough.

> As Freud himself asserted … is not the manufacturing of a substitute-formation, which recompenses the subject for his loss of reality, the most succinct definition of paranoiac construction as the subject's attempt to cure himself of the disintegration of his universe.[6]

Who is to ever know whether or not any cause is actually the true cause or not: this is exactly the same issue that faces any doctor: one can never tell exactly what the patient is suffering from; the diagnosis is based on the symptoms that the patient has. In this manner, one can always go to a doctor and merely display the symptoms in order to get either a medical certificate or some medicine that one desires. The doctor has no real recourse but to believe the patient: there is often no way of finding out. Even if a battery of tests were carried out on the patient, as long as (s)he maintains the performance of the symptoms, the illness is real. In this manner, medicine (and the law) are always dealing with performances, signs, the simulation of illness (and crime).

But even as the analyst, the doctor and the policeman are well aware of the simulation at hand, they will act accordingly. It is not so much that they have no choice (there is always a choice, the doctor can choose not to believe in the symptoms) but rather that there is no difference anymore (does it matter if the symptom is real or not; if the patient is displaying the symptoms, (s)he is incapacitated in the same manner as the real illness would).

And this is what is 'elementary': the reduction of the possibilities. This is the perfect crime: not the murder of reality by the killer, but rather by the policeman. The murder of the Real occurs at the moment the possibilities are strangled, leaving only one. This is the perverse core of the Law: each and every enactment of the Law (through a judgment, regardless of whether 'guilty' or 'non guilty') requires this blow to be struck, this murder to take place. This is why the arrest can never be made – for who will ever arrest her/ him self.[7]

---

[6] As read in Slavoj Zizek. (2000). *The Ticklish Subject.* pp.35.

[7] It is for this reason that a true detective will always face the full wrath of the Law. Recall the classic scene in all movies involving a good detective: "turn in your badge; you are suspended from the police force." It is only after this happens that the detective is free to make any real discovery: this is the moment in which (s)he will be able to enter the case (a mystery may be a more apt description of it) without any binds and true discoveries (new and un-predicted possibilities) can perhaps be made. This new discovery is only possible for it is no longer confined to the a priori context set by the Law. In some cases the true discovery is absolutely nothing – this must always be a possibility – and it is this possibility that the Law cannot subsume, and it is this that the Law will always seek to annihilate.

In some sense, the highest transgression that can be made in a court is to utter, "I don't know." For this reveals the perverse core of the courts which is that, not only is judgment impossible to pass on nothing, but more crucially that judgment itself – which has to be passed in any case, even when faced with the absolute un-knowing of "I don't know" – is based on nothing.

***

It is of absolutely no surprise that at the centre of the exhibition titled *The Changing Face of Terrorism* at the National Library in Singapore, lies a organizational chart of Jemaah Islamiah.[8] Whilst claiming that it is merely projected and hence speculative by nature, this does not change the fact that this is an attempt to conceive of the Jemaah Islamiah as an organization: literally a strategy of "organizing … by force in order to defeat it."

> Such is simulation, insofar as it is opposed to representation. Representation stems from the principle of the equivalence of the sign and the real (even if the equivalence is utopian, it is a fundamental axiom). Simulation, on the contrary, stems from the utopia of the principle of equivalence, from the radical negation of the sign as value, from the sign as the reversion and the death sentence of every reference. Whereas representation attempts to absorb simulation by interpreting it as a false representation, simulation envelopes the whole edifice of representation itself as a simulacrum.[9]

What happens with the organizational chart is the simulation of simulation: simulating the organization into existence in order that the organization can be dealt with: which is precisely the double simulation of creating a cause in order to deal with it. This takes the logic of Freud's "substitute formation" itself to its extreme: not only is the cause simulation such that the symptom can be arrested, but here the symptom itself is simulated such the cause is manufactured in order to deal with the 'symptom'.

Pontius Pilate asked the most precise question when he uttered "what is truth?" The only answer that suffices a question of that magnitude is not 'nothing', but 'absolutely everything': this is the seduction of the Real by the appearance of reality. And just like in all horror movies, the most terrifying moment is not when the mask is lifted to reveal a horrible face, but when the face beneath the mask is exactly the same as the mask itself. When one can no longer tell who the monster is, the monster is everywhere and everyone (yourself included).

Mc-Laden: would you like to super-size it?

In some way, the perfect brand has been created. Every single bomb that has gone off since September 11 2001 is credited to Osama bin Laden (whether directly or indirectly). Even when natural disasters strike, there is almost an automatic reaction to blame him, much in the same way that the Party could be blamed for bad weather in the old Soviet Union: bin Laden has taken over the role of the Absolute Other.

This works in a perfect way, as it is no longer only organizations which are fighting against states that use the name of bin Laden, but those very states as well. In this manner, all sides are relying on the brand of bin Laden in order to justify their actions (fighting in the name of God against the Great Satan; chasing 'terrorist

---

[8] The exhibition – *The Changing Face of Terrorism* - was held at the National Library in Singapore from 9 November to 17 December 2004.

[9] Jean Baudrillard. (1994). *Simulacra and Simulation.* pp.6.

organizations' and hunting them down because they are against freedom; insert any justification as desired). The name of bin Laden can accommodate anything and everything.

Osama bin Laden: the empty signifier: the perfect signifier.

The perfect brand: literally captured by the Adidas slogan, "Impossible is Nothing": there is nothing that cannot be attributed to the brand of bin Laden. In the eternal words of the seductress, bin Laden can "be anything you want me to be."[10]

Prosecutor:	And did you ask him about the term al-Qaeda?
FBI:	Yes we did.
Prosecutor:	And what did he say?
FBI:	He said that al-Qaeda was a *formula system* for what they carried out, talking about the bombing.
Prosecutor:	And did you ask him whether or not he'd heard of a group called al-Qaeda?
FBI:	We did.
Prosecutor:	And what did he say in response?
FBI:	He claimed that he'd never heard of a group called al-Qaeda.[11]

Al-Qaeda: an idea. Which everything else vortexes around. A perfect idea. Completely and utterly objectless. And completely and utterly empty: with full potentiality to be impregnated by any and every signified.

---

[10] An interesting consideration would be whether bin Laden has reached iconic status. To begin with one has to consider if there is a difference between an icon and a brand (Marilyn Monroe is an icon; Nike is a brand) or if an icon a particular status (Michael Jordan has reached iconic status because not only is he known in the world of basket-ball – that would only be strong branding – but beyond it). In either case, it is indisputable that Osama bin Laden is known beyond the circle of 'terrorist organizations' (whatever that means). In fact, bin Laden is so well known that his circle of influence defies boundaries any longer.

The possible distinction between 'brand' and 'icon' was brought to my attention in a conversation with Esther Tan. (1 December, 2005): Singapore.

[11] Jason Burke. (2003). *Al-Qaeda: Casting a Shadow of Terror.* pp.12. *Italics* from source.

This sequence was taken from the chapter "What is Al Qaeda?" The 'he' in question is K.K. Muhammed, who was allegedly involved with Osama bin Laden's network. Burke attempts to establish that Al-Qaeda is not so much an organization but an idea (or a formula in his terms) that was used as operating ideas for disparate groups of people. In this sense, network is the precise term here: the disparate groups were a network formed around an idea called Al-Qaeda.

Bush vs S&M: torture is fine; images of torture on the other hand ...

A new war has begun in the United States: a witch-hunt of the sex industry, in particular the segment of the industry that involves any depiction of pain or torture, for instance, sex workers in the S&M industry and producers of videos or websites that portray explicit signs of dominance (Max Hardcore has been particularly persecuted, along with many website which are S&M themed). In response many websites have taken down any photos which they deem may draw attention from the administration for fear of persecution: a clear sign that the Bush administration is winning this particular campaign is the manner in which pre-emptive self-censorship is taking place.

The most obvious way of looking at this (the typical conservative reaction) would be that the culture of S&M runs contrary to the morals and the values of the predominantly Judeo-Christian US. And thus in this manner, all the Bush administration is doing is protecting the values of the majority by clamping down on the aberrant few.

A more interesting twist would be that S&M (and torture by extension) is a practice of the Other and not of the US. In this way, it is okay if others do it – which is why torture is fine in Guantanamo Bay (after all the Cubans are not morally upright Americans; they are merely soul-less Communists) but not on American soil. Everything can be tolerated, patronizingly of course, as long as it is not 'civilized' Americans who are indulging in this type of behavior.[12]

If torture is the activity of the Other, then by definition, any display of it must not be found on homeland: God forbid if Americans actually find pleasure in such depravity. A crackdown against all such displays (in this regard who cares if most of the sex industry is merely displaying images; who can tell the difference anyway) is an attempt to cover up the fact that torture is not merely an activity of the Other, but very much a part of the culture of the US itself. For sans this 'arrest' of the images of S&M (and by a wider definition images of 'torture' and pain), the logical conclusion would be that the use of torture is not merely a foreign phenomenon: one can no longer use the excuse that the American soldiers in a foreign land were 'infected' with un-American thoughts and actions. In fact, the tortures at both Abu Gharib and Guantanamo Bay were not anomalies but merely manifestations of the American way of life.

The horror is generated when the very logic in which we operate on is revealed. It is upon this over-loading of any system (by taking it to its own logical extremes), that the Real jumps out at us. We have played out the fantasy of planes crashing into buildings hundreds of times in Hollywood movies. The event of September 11 had such a profound effect on us, not because it could actually happen (we've always known it to be possible), but because we were horrified when our fantasies came true: when the gap is bridged, when fantasy is fulfilled, we do not get jouissance but instead a nightmare situation (literally of the Real jumping out at us).

---

[12] This is the only reason why the revelations of the pictures at Abu Gharib were such a shock to the American public. It was not the shock that the US tortured the enemy (who didn't know that), but the fact that fellow Americans were seen taking pleasure in the torturing.

The (deadly) exchange

At the point of arrest, of stopping the symptom, what has happened is the subsumption of the event under the categories of the subject. In effect, what the subject has done is to imbue the event with her/ his own meaning (impregnated the signifier with a privileged signified). This is when the ghost of the Enlightenment not only haunts us but possesses us, with detrimental effects. For at the moment in which meaning is imbued into the event, it is injected back into the realm of exchange: we are no longer dealing in the realm of stakes any longer; we are now in the realm of raising exchange value, a deadly game of one-upsmanship. What this translates to is a game played with the actual bodies of people: the realm of stakes remained purely symbolic, but the realm of exchange requires real objects (make no mistake, people are the objects with which this game is played).

The refusal to allow terror to be what it is – a pure effect sans meaning – has this consequence: when a state encounters the death of a 'terrorist' (say a suicide bomber), what other recourse is there but to increase the deaths on their own side (in an exchange, one must always match with a surplus). We see this very logic playing out in Iraq and Afghanistan: you kill one of ours, we kill at least 2 of yours (and by the same logic; one of yours die, 2 of ours must die).

"Impossible is Nothing" – the Adidas slogan that perfectly captures the logic of globalization. Everything can be done: everything can be exchanged: everything can be (re)produced (infinitely). And it is this refusal to allow for the singularity of objects – the impossible exchange – that is threatening to over-whelm us. By flattening everything – this is the obsession with accountability that is being called for; transparency – we have entered ourselves into this realm of exchange. If "impossible is nothing," every (exchange) is now possible: this is the utopia of the global village. And just like every utopia that is fulfilled, the outcome is far from jouissance, but instead, a nightmare.

Narrating the Other into existence

The strategy of all nation states is the strategy of war. And in every war, one needs an enemy, the Other. And it is this that all states are desperate to create: no one cares whether this Other exists or not, no one ever did. In this "war on terror" an enemy is required and the enemy will be found (regardless of whether (s)he is there in the first place).

This is the last desperate cry of the nation state: de-territorialization has occurred in such a massive form (this is globalization's triumphant sprint towards the finish line) that it is no longer governments but multi-national corporations that run the world. Is it then any wonder that nation states are unable to cope with the idea that is Al-Qaeda. This must have been how the Polish army felt in World War II when they led a cavalry charge against the German panzer divisions; war had completely changed and it was a last symbolic (and completely futile) attempt. But at least they were still fighting on the same battle field – the mechanisms of war might have changed, but at least then they had the same parameters (over-run the enemy and take their territory). Hence, there was still a chance (no matter how faint) that the Polish horses might win. But now the nation state is fighting a war in which it there is no enemy left: the field has completely disappeared. And in its last act of desperation, the nation state is attempting to re-territorialize (not just bring

49

subjects back into the fold, but more radically the very idea of the nation itself). This is why the idea of the Other is so desperately clung to: the nation state cannot exist sans the Other, the enemy.[13] We see this most clearly on September 12 2001: never has the idea of the United States of America been as strong as the day after the absolute enemy, the absolute Other, was narrated into existence.

The strategy is the same as it has always been: narrate the enemy as the invading force, the virus that encroaches on the Self and introduces itself into the system. "Terrorists are like vermin," the now infamous phrase by Bush Jr., captures this strategy best – it is exactly the same rhetorical strategy that is used when talking about immigrants, particular forms of drugs, cancer and AIDS.[14] This is the lesson of Hitler that remained with us – there is no stronger force that draws people together than a common enemy: "the enemy of my enemy is my friend."

You are MY monster: give me back my name.

It is of absolutely no coincidence that a common error in literature is the mistaken identity of Mary Shelley's monster. The fact that quite a number of people have re-named the monster after his creator suggests that there are two Frankensteins: since Victor Frankenstein did create the monster, it is not inconceivable that it takes on his family name. What makes it more interesting though, is that when pressed for the scientist's name, the same people tend not to be able to name him. In this way, not only has the monster taken Victor's name, he has now stripped him of his identity.

In much the same way, the Other that we have narrated into existence – the virus that we have put the blame on in order to white-wash the fact that violence is inherently written into the fabric of the modern state[15] – returns to haunt us.

This is due to the fact that we did not count on our envy of this very Other that we created. In narrating them as the savage Other (the one who relies on violence; the very violence that we as 'civilized' people have rejected), in particular as fundamentalists, who are driven by a singular belief and are willing to achieve it at all costs, and even in prescribing ridiculous explanations for their actions (the

---

[13] In "Narrating the Nation" found in Homi Bhabha. (1990). *Nation and Narration.* Bhabha argues that the Other is the crucial narrative for the existence of a nation. For instance, the concept of India does not exist without the idea of Pakistan. This is especially true when you consider that experientially, no one living in India believes in this idea anymore: people living there identify with their state rather than the nation (though conceptually the idea of the Other remains the same; Gujarat only means anything because of the other states around it). The only time when the concept of India is strong is when a cricket match is on: that is because the absolute Other in cricket is fulfilled by its great enemy, Pakistan.

[14] Susan Sontag traces the discourse on cancer, and more recently AIDS, and notes that they have always been depicted as a foreign (this is the key, it is always the Other that is the cause of all the problems) virus, that has invaded the body (of the Self). Some of Sontag's work on this include "Illness as Metaphor" (1979) and "AIDS and its Metaphors" (1989).

In *Crack Wars*, Avital Ronell traces the discourse of the 'war on drugs' in the United States as an attempt to police particular cultures and discourses that run contrary to the official discourse. To read this excellent meditation in full, please see Avital Ronell. (2004). *Crack Wars: Literature Addiction Mania.*

[15] The very logic of the social contract is premised on the surrendering of the monopoly of violence (at least in terms of legitimated violence) to the state: violence is the very basis of the Law. Why else would Justice be carrying a sword in her hands?

most popular at the moment seems to be the 72 virgins awaiting the martyrs in heaven), what we did not realize is that we have prescribed upon them our very own lack: Belief.

In this post-ideological age (the death knell was struck when we began to claim that everything is political),[16] it is this very ability to believe in something that truly scares us. It is for this reason that there was an outcry against the Taliban for blowing up the statues of Buddha in Afghanistan: it was not as if the West suddenly became Buddhist and believed in the sanctity of the statues, but rather, the outrage was a reaction to the audacity of the Taliban openly displaying their belief in their religion. This is almost a case of 'how dare they actually believe', which really translates to, 'I wish I still had this ability to believe; how dare they believe when I no longer can.'[17]

This is the same reason why the suicide bomber remains such an enigma for us: we can no longer conceive of anyone that is willing to believe in, let alone give up her/ his life for, anything. And it is this enigma – this that we cannot grasp, cannot subsume, under our categories of 'understanding' – that truly makes us tremble, that terrifies us. After all, when one is willing to give up one's life, what defence is there any longer?

The Revenge of the Other

The nation state narrates the Other into existence in order to create the conditions of war, via the creation of an enemy, which would legitimize its own existence. What it did not count on was the refusal of the Other to fight on its own terms: the refusal to engage on a dialectic realm.

For the Other realized that it is precisely the hinge on which the concept of the nation state rests. So it takes its perfect revenge by disappearing – by refusing to be, by refusing to play by the same rules. And in this manner, the Other has disappeared completely into the Self: the Self and the Other have become exactly the same – completely indistinguishable. The mirror is now the Self: the term 'mirror image' is now completely moot: we are our own mirror.

This is why terror scares us so much. For if there is no Other left, then we are our own Other. There is no enemy. We are the enemy.

> The perfect assassination is when you kill off someone, and live as him so no one ever notices that he's dead.[18]

---

[16] At the very moment that we claimed that everything is political, we have moved into the realm of the trans-political: in fact, all concepts have moved into the realm of the 'trans' now (trans-economic: everything is economics, trans-social: everything is a social concern; ad infinitum, ad nauseum). When this occurs, everything becomes completely and utterly exchangeable: everything is political or economic or social – all categories cease to have any meaning whatsoever and move into the realm of the pure signifier.

[17] This analysis is inspired by Zizek and can be found amongst other places in *The Puppet and the Dwarf*.

[18] This phrase was uttered by Kenny Png. (2 December, 2005): Singapore in a discussion about the film *The Talented Mr. Ripley*.

But is this not also already the murder of your Self? In this sense, this is not only the perfect crime, the also the perfect double murder in which no one will ever be caught. And like every crime scene, when no one is caught (who cares if the right person is caught, as long as someone is), the fear remains forever: (s)he is still somewhere out there.

"What is to be done": this is the question but when asked is it still a question?

We ask this question as far as this question can even begin to be asked. Or perhaps more accurately, we ask this question as a pure question, a question sans a known answer, without an available answer, without any reference that one can be draw from. In this manner, we have to ask the question in the true revolutionary sense of Lenin (which ironically was not the manner in which he uttered the phrase): a spontaneous eruption in which the outcome is always already unknown. For perhaps only in this instance is there the potentiality for a new occurrence, a new rupture, to take place.[1]

But first, in order to even ask the question, we must put the question aside: we must first meditate on exactly what we are asking the question of. (One can not ask a question 'about'; in doing so, one has already framed the context and in that way, the answer is already plotted in the question. This is what is meant by the age old phrase, "the question begets the answer"). When one asks a question 'of', there is no a priori frame set for the answer: it is a question in its full potentiality.

Since we are asking the question of terror, then we must ask of it sans subsuming it under our own frames (as far as this is even possible, for the violence of langue always already attempt to do this). In this way, we might be able to escape this fate by giving up the notion of a solution – and in doing so, all we might (for 'will' is always already too certain) unveil are possibilities.[2] Even though there is a distinct possibility that nothing might happen, nothing might be unveiled, it is only in this manner that we can accord the true status of an event to the occurrence (which happens in a time and space). And it is only in this manner that we maintain the hope of separating terror from the cycle of violence, for if the separation does not occur, then there will just be an unending sequence of violence, each time with the stakes raised – and one must never forget that human lives are the stakes here – in an brutal game of one-upsmanship. It is only through the acknowledgment of the true status of the event (which is the site of violence) that can one then begin to meditate on terror itself.

But first we must digress in order to address a crucial issue: if "understanding is in want of understanding,"[3] does this in-comprehension, and incomprehensibility, that resides in each and every event necessitate that nothing can (or 'must') be done? This is akin to the standard critique of post-modernity: in the unearthing of endless possibilities, this then makes any action impossible (for that would merely be privileging one and marginalizing all the other possibilities). However that misses

---

[1] But of course with potentiality always already lies the potentiality not to be. Which is why in every true revolution, there is a potentiality of non-actualization. Perhaps it is this possibility of the 'not' that allows for a real change to occur – for if actualization was guaranteed, the outcome is by definition known (something will happen) and if known a priori, it will be subsumed by the hegemonic thought. This is the fate that befalls most 'revolutions': the fixation on an outcome (which by definition must be calculable with goals, aims, outcomes, failures, success, repeatability) guarantees that it is subsumed under the logic of reproduction and capital once again.

[2] And just as we 'unveil' there is always already a concealment that is taking place. This is the profundity of 'aletheia': the truth that is always already (n)either revealing (n)or concealing itself. Perhaps if we approach 'terror' from this angle, there might be hope for something new.

[3] Werner Hamacher. (1996). *Premises: Essays in Philosophy and Literature from Kant to Celan.* pp.1.

out on the crucial aspect of decisions (and any accompanying action): all decisions require an moment of madness. And it is only in this manner that we can retain any hope of an ethical decision: if decisions were made solely based on a 'rational deduction' then there would not be any measure of responsibility left in them (that was the only thing that must be done; what sort of choice is there then?). It is only through the acknowledgment that the decision made inevitably privileges a particular course of action (whilst marginalizing all the other possibilities) that the true weight of the decision is brought to bear. And only with this weight of the marginalized bearing on the Subject, can (s)he be said to be truly responsible for that decision (one always already has to answer to the possibilities that were left out).[4]

This is the difficult problem that the New-Age vegetarians are trying to dodge. Their claim is that they refuse to eat any animal for that is engaging in the murder of a life. And therefore, the solution they have is to eat only plants. This is an extremely obscene solution, for it does not acknowledge that plants are living things as well (just because you don't know if they suffer in death does not mean that they don't: that is a truly anthropocentric argument). In order to respond to the full brevity of the situation, one has to accept that all plants and animals are living things. Hence death is inscribed into every meal. Which leaves us with two options: either we choose not to eat at all (and starve as a result; which still doesn't free us from the cycle of death), or we accept the full responsibility that each of our meals is a result of murders.

The lesson of Freddy Krueger

If terror is an effect, then we must address it as such (and not as a cause). In this sense, it is a treatment of symptoms that we are seeking and not an absolute 'cure'; there is no search for the root (transcendental) cause for there is none. Terror is the effect of a simulation of violence and not violence itself. An attempt to 'cure' the violence would only lead to more violence, and it is this that we must avoid. Perhaps we must learn a lesson from both the doctor and the policeman and not least of all, Freddy Krueger.

When Freddy kills you in your sleep you die in real life. The usual reading of this is that there is no distinction between real(ity) and the Real, in that reality (the dream state) slips into the Real. Conversely one could read *A Nightmare on Elm Street*[5] as the Real being the dream state (we live in a simulated reality and the Real only occurs in our subconscious). However a more interesting consideration would be, perhaps the deaths of Freddy's victims occur at the very moment they realize that their fantasy of being killed by Freddy comes true (after all who living on Elm Street had not heard of Freddy). In this sense, it is not Freddy who comes after them; it is they themselves who summon their own deaths: this is why speaking about Freddy (reproducing the signifier that is Freddy) is the most dangerous thing

---

[4] This also challenges the absoluteness of any decision, for it exposes the fact that each decision always already rests on less than stable foundations: ultimately there is no legitimate reason for any decision above another. By extension, this makes any transcendental claim impossible as well; or that it always puts a decision on a transcendental level: the reason for the decision is always already illegitimate, based on nothing but an assumption that cannot be justified within the parameters of the decision itself. This inability to justify any transcendental claim was beautifully articulated by Derrida when he said, "I cannot prove nor disprove the existence of God. What I can do is to challenge anyone [or any institution] that uses God to make an absolute claim."

[5] The *A Nightmare on Elm Street* series began in 1984 and was written and directed by Wes Craven.

one can do on Elm Street. Their corresponding death(s) – in 'real life' – is the moment which the horror of the Real confronts them; the point in which the fantasy comes true (the "nightmare" in the title is truly apt in this case). What is truly fascinating is the manner in which the to-be-victims then choose to combat Freddy. In order to kill Freddy they completely ignore the fact that there is no Object that is causing their deaths (it is they themselves who are summoning Freddy in the first place), and combat the effect (the manifestation of Freddy in their dreams) head on. This strategy is one which recognizes Freddy Krueger is merely an effect sans cause, and it is in this realm that the battle must take place.

***

In the heart of Singapore lies a shopping centre called Wisma Atria and there is a link-way between the subway system and the building. At the entrance of that particular link-way, sits a 'security guard' (this began about two weeks after September 11th). The security guard merely sits there: he does not stop anyone, check anyone's baggage; in fact he does absolutely nothing.

In short, he is the perfect symbol of security in this age of terror.

The Wisma guard – the perfect simulation of security. Just like the doctor that treats the symptom in order to arrest it, the Wisma guard performs the sign of security to perfection: completely object-less security. Unlike airport security (or the ridiculous idea of 'Air Marshals'), who actually attempt to address the 'cause' of terror (of which there is absolutely none) which then has detrimental results: just look at the recent case of Air Marshals shooting an innocent man who was mentally unstable just because he was exhibiting signs of terroristic behavior.[6] (When it is an Objectless 'cause' it is then a master signifier for now any 'cause' can now be the cause; we move into the realm of 'simulated causes', with very real results).

In fact, the current situation of attempting to deal with the 'cause' of terror, and by doing so simulating an Objectless cause (which then will never go away),[7] what is ensured is that a simulated effect will forever take hold. At the moment, not only do airline passengers have to fear being blown up by 'terrorist suicide bombers', they also have to fear being shot by Air Marshals: the 'cause' has evaporated into nothingness, the 'effect' has moved into the realm of ubiquity.

---

[6] On 7 December 2005, in Orlando Miami, Rigoberto Alpizar was killed by an Air Marshal after displaying signs 'consistent' with terroristic behavior. Whilst it is easy (and overly convenient) to condemn the Air Marshal for his actions, it is actually impossible to distinguish the signs of terror from an actual 'terrorist' (this is assuming there is an actuality to begin with). This is best captured by the sign that is on display at American airports: "Jokes about hijacking planes are not funny. It is a Federal Offence and you will be prosecuted."

Of course the brutal irony is that only after the Kennedy assassination have presidential assassinations been classified as federal offences (they used to be state offences). Which is a crucial move as it then reconfigures the presidential assassination from an event (a killing in a specific time and place) to one sans an actual location (it is now a killing that happens all over the nation at the same time; perhaps on television screens). Perhaps this is the ultimate admission that it is the re-production of the assassination that is more important that the actual death of the person; after Kennedy, there is no longer a president, only the image of a president. Kennedy's assassination in Dallas was the US's requiem to politics.

[7] There is nothing more horrifying than the monster that cannot be identified, nothing that scares us more than an Objectless monster. For if there was an Object, one could actually deal with it; the Objectless nature of this 'cause' (which does not exist in the first place) ensures its immortality.

***

To counter the effects of cigarette advertising (the growing number of smokers), many states have been resorting to facts and figures. Most of the campaigns (whilst using the same medium of print and television advertising) focus on the consequences of smoking (dying of cancer, affecting the health of your family, and the people around you, etc). This is an attempt to get to the 'root cause' of smoking – the bare facts – and show smokers why it is such a bad idea for them to light up.

What the campaigns have completely missed is the fact that everyone already knows this. It is not that smokers light up due to ignorance of the facts, but in-spite[8] of them. In this light, it is not surprising that the only anti-smoking campaign that ever worked was the one that featured the Marlboro Man with a limp cigarette (the tagline was: "Smoking causes impotence"). It was not the fact (impotence) that allowed this particular campaign to have its 'desired effects' (who doesn't know that smoking can cause impotence) but the fact that it attacked the very signified of the Marlboro Man (alpha maleness). In this manner, it arrests the effects of the Marlboro Man campaign (and perhaps cigarette advertising in general for the Marlboro Man is the master image) whilst ignoring 'root causes' totally; this is the reason for its effectiveness.

***

On January 15 2004, on the front page of *TODAY* (a national newspaper in Singapore) the names of alleged members of Jemaah Islamiah and the Moro Islamic Liberation Front were published.[9] However only their names were released sans pictures nor any other form of information or identification: in other words, only the signifiers were released, without any referentiality whatsoever. No one has actually been alerted of their identities; even their employers remain in the dark and they will be free to continue with their daily lives and jobs. An epiphany when it comes to state policy and news – a realization that terror only exists in the realm of the news and has no relation to the world.

---

[8] Perhaps the root 'spite' requires more attention that I have given it here. For there are a large number of smokers who will continue smoking due to the fact that everyone is telling them not to: one of the main components of the advertisements by cigarette manufacturers is 'individuality.' Who cares if the 'individuality' has been commodified: who can tell the difference anyway.

In many ways, Cypher from *The Matrix* captures it best when he says: "You know, I know this steak doesn't exist. I know that when I put it in my mouth, the Matrix is telling my brain that it is juicy and delicious. After nine years, you know what I realize? [*Takes a bite of steak*]. Ignorance is bliss."

What Cypher does not realize is just how conservative he is being when he utters those lines. For it is not that "ignorance is bliss" but that there is absolutely no difference between having a steak that is really "juicy and delicious" and when your brain tells you that it is so.

[9] Teo Hwee Nak. "A smaller brush with terror and a lighter price to pay." (January 15, 2004). In *TODAY* pp.1.

Hyper-terror or happiness is a warm gun

To conquer death you only have to die/ You only have to die.[10]

The age of revolution has passed: revolutions are merely revolving nowadays. A perverse reading of the 'eternal return of the same' seems to be the legacy that has been bequeathed us, and it is this that continues to haunt us. For it is not that the 'eternal return of the same' does not unveil a difference every single time, but that this difference has always already been subsumed by the logic of capital: the transparency of globalization and its flattening out of difference guarantees that there is nothing beyond the same that reappears (and is reproduced) every single time. The triumph of capital is not that it is a perfect logic that encompasses everything; capital's strategy is the exact opposite – a completely meaningless logic that sutures everything else; the perfect seducer which says: "I can be anything you want me to be."

It is this non-meaning that the spectre of terror has adopted. The perfect foil to globalization which guarantees the continuation of globalization: capital's perfect strategy in order to continue the fantasy forever: a radical strategy of non-fulfillment.

In order to subvert the strategy of capital, an even more radical strategy is needed. A subversion that does not attempt to counter this non-meaning, for this would only succeed in introducing meaning into the fray, meaning that would be subsumed back into the very logic of globalization itself, but a subversion of non-meaning itself.

> To seduce is to appear weak. To seduce is to render weak. We seduce with our weakness, never with strong signs or powers. In seduction, we enact this weakness, and this is what gives seduction its strength.

> We seduce with our death, our vulnerability, and with the void that haunts us. The secret is to know how to play with death in the absence of a gaze or gesture, in the absence of knowledge or meaning.[11]

We must offer ourselves up in this game of stakes, this game of one-upmanship, for the effects (terror in this case) only have effect when there is resistance. Just like the Foucaultian 'dispositif', it assumes that the resistance of the Subject: sans resistance there is absolutely no disciplinary measure to the mechanism. It is in this light that the phrase "the happiest slave is the one who thinks he is free" must be taken extremely seriously. In fact to be even more radical, we should re-word the phrase as, 'the slave who thinks he is free is happy, precisely because he is free.'

In order for the complete separation of terror and violence to occur, we must take terror to its extreme. Terror is not enough: we need hyper-terror to take place. We must allow terror to consume us to such an extent that it no longer consumes us.

---

[10] Andrew Lloyd-Webber & Tim Rice. (1970). "Poor Jerusalem" in *Jesus Christ Superstar*.

[11] Jean Baudrillard. (1990). *Seduction*. pp.83.

And just like the perverse freedom that is found in Fascist and Totalitarian states, it is this allowing the Self to be consumed by the (Absolute) Other that will grant us our freedom from terror. In some sense, the slogan to live by now is not 'be afraid of nothing' but rather 'be afraid of absolutely everything for fear will set you free.'

Freddy Krueger was probably the last 'monster' to ever frighten us. We have seen so many 'monsters' appear on the screen that now whenever 'monsters' appear, not only is there no fear but in fact their appearance is usually greeted with laughter. In fact, nowadays, the only movies that truly frighten us are the ones sans any monster; the possibility of monsters is what truly scares us still (hence the popularity of Asian horror movies). This is what Marx meant when he said that history repeats itself "the first time as a tragedy, the second time as a comedy."[12] Repetition ad infinitum; as the farce becomes more and more farcical it eventually becomes pure repetition (where the entire point of repetition is repetition itself) – sans meaning and sans effect.

Hence every single terror warning must be taken with the utmost seriousness: it is no longer the sense of detached irony that will save us: instead we have to now immerse in the sign with the utmost earnestness, and perhaps in this surplus of reality, this sur-real gesture, we might actually manage to overload the signifier of terror, leaving the sign not so much meaningless, but rather overly-impregnated with meaning. Both meaninglessness and a surplus of meaning have the same effect in terms of signification, but are completely different when it comes to significance: the absence of meaning leaves the signifier in perfect potentiality whilst the surplus of meaning leaves it impotent.

Just about every state has a manifestation of a sign that reads "please report any suspicious article." If everyone took that sign utterly seriously, nothing would ever work again, especially the sign itself. It is this distancing from the complete seriousness of the sign that allows terror to maintain a hold of our imagination – a perversion of the hopeful "all power to the imagination"[13] – and that is what allows terror to still have any real results (through the maintaining of its link with violence): just look at how difficult it is to locate a refuse bin in any train station after the Madrid bombings (it is not due to the fact that refuse bins were used in the Madrid bombings so removing them is a precautionary measure, because no one will use them again; it would be too obvious. Moreover monitoring bins via CCTV would be more effective. The removal of refuse bins is due to the fact that in our imagination, refuse bins in train stations have become the signifier for bombs and it is this that continues to haunt us. Removing them does absolutely nothing – in fact the absence of refuse bins will forever cement the signified of bombs in the minds of everyone). It is in this manner that groups engaged in violence, and (nation) states, have effects over us: by exacting power over our imagination which has been captured by the link between violence and terror; the link that is maintained by our distancing from terror.

---

[12] Karl Marx. (1852). *The Eighteenth Brumaire of Louis Bonaparte.* pp.7.

In some versions 'comedy' is translated as 'farce.' Either translation does not hamper the point being made here.

[13] This phrase was scribbled on the walls of the Sorbonne in May 1968 and is usually attributed to Paul Virilio.

By allowing terror to envelope us, and utterly consume us, we do not drown in violence and death, but rather seduce terror with its very own rules: utter and complete meaninglessness, a meaninglessness that is not empty, but that is precisely too much.[14]

---

[14] By plunging into terror, we spin it beyond referentiality, beyond the stakes of human life and death, and perhaps address it in its own realm, a realm beyond life and death, beyond good and evil, perhaps beyond everything but terror itself.

> The absolute rule, that of symbolic exchange, is to return what you received. Never less, but always more. The absolute rule of thought is to return the world as we received it: unintelligible. And if it is possible, to return it a little bit more unintelligible. A little bit more enigmatic. (Jean Baudrillard: "Radical Thought")

For it is only by thinking the singularity of terror as singular, unknowable, undefinable, enigmatic, that prevents it from being a totalizing concept, one that effaces us. It is this unknowability, this gap that re-opens the space for negotiation – for violence – not outside of terror, but within terror itself that gives us hope.

Echoes

Agamben, Giorgio. (1998). *Homo Sacer: Sovereign Power and Bare Life*. (Daniel Heller-Roazen, Trans.). Stanford: Meridian.
_____. (1999). *Potentialities: Collected Essays in Philosophy*. (Daniel Heller-Roazen, Trans.). Stanford: Meridian.
Althusser, Louis. (1977). "Ideology and the State" in *Lenin and Philosophy and Other Essays*. (B. Brewster, Trans.). London: New Left Books.
Badiou, Alain. (2002). *Ethics: an Essay on the Understanding of Evil*. (Peter Hallward, Trans.). London: Verso.
_____. (2003). *Infinite Thought: Truth and the Return of Philosophy*. (Oliver Feltham & Justin Clemens, Trans.). London: Continuum.
Barthes, Roland. (1977). *Image, Music, Text*. (Stephen Heath, Ed. and Trans.). New York: Hill.
_____. (1996). *Mythologies*. (Annette Levers, Trans.). London: Vintage.
Baudrillard, Jean. (1988). *The Ecstasy of Communication*. (Caroline Schutze, Trans.). New York: Semiotext(e)
_____. (1990). *Seduction*. (Brian Singer, Trans.). New York: St Martin's Press.
_____. (1994). *Simulacra and Simulation*. (Sheila F. Glazer, Trans.). Ann Arbor: The University of Michigan Press.
_____. (1995). *The Gulf War did not take place*. (Paul Patton, Trans.). Bloomington: Indiana University Press.
_____. (1999). *The Transparency of Evil: Essays in Extreme Phenomena*. (James Benedict, Trans.). London: Verso.
_____. (2001). *Impossible Exchange*. (Chris Turner, Trans.). London: Verso.
_____. (2002). *The Spirit of Terrorism*. (Chris Turner, Trans.). London: Verso.
_____. (2002). *The Perfect Crime*. (Chris Turner, Trans.). London: Verso.
_____. (2005). *The System of Objects*. (James Benedict, Trans.). London: Verso.
_____. (2005). *The Intelligence of Evil or the Lucidity Pact*. (Chris Turner, Trans.). Oxford: Berg Publishers.
Bhabha, Homi. (1990). *The Nation and Narration*. London: Routledge.
Borradori, Giovanna. (2003). *Philosophy in a Time of Terror: Dialogues with Jurgen Habermas and Jacques Derrida*. (Luis Guzman, Pascale-Anne Brault & Michael Naas, Trans.). Chicago: The University of Chicago Press.
Brunton, Finn. (2005). *Decontrol in Science, Music and War*. MA Thesis. Saas Fee: European Graduate School.
Burke, Jason. (2003). *Al-Qaeda: Casting a Shadow of Terror*. London: I.B. Tauris.
Cixous, Helene. (1976). "The Laugh of the Medusa" in *Signs*, Vol. 1, No. 4. (Keith Cohen & Paula Cohen, Trans.). Chicago: University of Chicago Press. pp. 875-93.
_____. (2004). *Portrait of Jacques Derrida as a Young Jewish Saint*. (Beverly Bie Brahic, Trans.). New York: Columbia University Press.
_____. (2005). *Stigmata*. London: Routledge.
Choi, Jooyong. (2007). *The Grotesque Body: Past and Present*. Seoul: Ewha Women's University – Provincializing English: The English Department in the Asian Context.
Deleuze, Gilles. (1993). *The Fold: Leibniz and the Baroque*. (Tom Conley, Trans.). Minnesota: University of Minnesota Press.

_____. (1999). *Coldness and Cruelty.* (Jean McNeil, Trans.). New York: Zone Books.

_____. (2002). *Pure Immanence: Essays on A Life.* (Anne Boyman, Trans.). New York: Zone Books.

Deleuze, Gilles. & Guattari, Felix. (1977). *Anti-Oedipus: Capitalism and Schizophrenia.* (Helen Lane, Mark Seem, & Robert Hurley, Trans.). New York: Penguin.

_____. (1987). *A Thousand Plateaus: Capitalism and Schizophrenia.* (Brian Massumi, Trans.). Minnesota: University of Minnesota Press.

Delilio, Don. (1999). *White Noise.* Hammondsworth: Penguin Books.

Derrida, Jacques. (1996). *The Gift of Death.* (David Wills, Trans.). Chicago: The University of Chicago Press.

_____. (1997). *Of Grammatology.* (Gayatri C. Spivak, Trans.). Baltimore: The John Hopkins University Press.

_____. (1998). *Right of Inspection.* (David Wills, Trans.). New York: The Monacelli Press.

_____. (2001). *On Cosmopolitanism and Forgiveness.* (Mark Dooley & Michael Hughes, Trans.). London: Routledge.

_____. (2005). *Rogues: Two Essays on Reason.* (Pascale-Anne Brault & Michael Naas, Trans.). Stanford: Meridian.

Derrida, Jacques. & Roudinesco, Elizabeth. (2004). *For What Tomorrow: a Dialogue.* (Jeff Fort, Trans.). Stanford: Stanford University Press.

Fabian, Johannes. (1983). *Time and the Other: How Anthropology makes its Object.* New York: Columbia University Press.

Fernando, Jeremy. (2005). 'Auto-replay: The Perversion of Journalism' in *LittleGirlOnline: a magazine of tactical thinking (vol2).*

_____. (2006). 'The Spectre of the National that Haunts Singapore (Cinema) or You Can Only See Ghosts if You are Blind' in *borderlands e-journal (vol5:3).*

Fynsk, Christopher. (2000). *Infant Figures: The Death of the Infans and Other Scenes of Origin.* Stanford: Stanford University Press.

Gramsci, Antonio. (1971). *Selections from Prison Notebooks.* (Q. Hoare, & G.N. Smith, Trans.). London: Laurence & Wishart.

Hamacher, Werner. (1999). *Premises: Essays on Philosophy and Literature from Kant to Celan.* (Peter Fenves, Trans.). Stanford: Meridian.

_____. (2007). *Uncalled: A Note on Kafka's 'Test'.* Saas Fee: Open Lecture at the European Graduate School.

Hölzl, Julia. (2007). *Beyond Eden [distorting symmetree].* Munich: Grin.

Jarry, Alfred. (1997). *The Ubu Plays: Ubu roi, Ubu cocu, Ubu enchaine & Ubu sur la butte.* (Kenneth McLeish, Trans.). London: Nick Hern Books.

Kierkegaard, Soren. (1997). *The Seducer's Diary.* (Howard V. Hong, Trans). Princeton: Princeton University Press.

Latour, Bruno. (1999). *Pandora's Hope: Essays on the Reality of Science Studies.* Cambridge: Harvard University Press.

Lippmann, Walter. (1922). *Public Opinion.* New York: Harcourt, Brace and Co.

Lyotard, Jean-Francois. (1984). *The Postmodern Condition: A Report on Knowledge.* (Geoff Bennington, & Brian Massumi, Trans.). Minneapolis: University of Minnesota Press.

Lyotard, Jean-Francois. & Thebaud, Jean-Loup. (1985). *Just Gaming.* (Wlad Godzich, Trans.). Minnesota: University of Minnesota Press.

Lucretius. (2005). *Sensation and Sex.* (R.E. Latham, Trans.). London: Penguin.

McLuhan, Marshall. & Fiore, Quentin. (1967). *The Medium is the Massage: an Inventory of Effects.* New York: Bantam.

Marquis de Sade. (2000). *Philosophy in the Boudoir.* (Meredith X, Trans.). New York: Creation Books.

Nietzsche, Friedrich. (1967). *The Birth of Tragedy.* (Walter Kaufmann, Trans.). New York: Vintage Books.

_____. (1967). *The Case of Wagner.* (Walter Kaufmann, Trans.). New York: Vintage Books.

_____. (1989). *On The Genealogy of Morals.* (Walter Kaufmann & R.J. Hollingdale, Trans.). New York: Vintage Books.

Ronell, Avital. (1998). *Finitude's Score: Essays for the End of the Millennium.* Nebraska: University of Nebraska Press.

_____.(2003). *Stupidity.* Chicago: University of Illinois Press.

_____. (2004). *Crack Wars: Literature Addiction Mania.* Chicago: University of Illinois Press.

_____. (2005). *The Test Drive.* Chicago: University of Illinois Press.

Schirmacher, Wolfgang. (1994). "Homo Generator: Media and Postmodern Technology" in G. Bender., & T. Duckrey. (Eds.). *Culture on the Brink: Ideologies of Technology.* New York: The New Press.

_____. (2000). "Cloning Humans with Media: Impermanence and Imperceptible Perfection" in *Poiesis 2.* Toronto: EGS Press.

_____. (2001). "Netculture" in *Poiesis 3.* Toronto: EGS Press.

Su, Cui. (2006). *Is Third Cinema Dead?* Unpublished manuscript.

Shah, Idries. (1974). *Reflections: Fables in the Sufi Tradition.* New York: Penguin Books.

Tan, See Kam. & Fernando, Jeremy. (2007). "The Singapore in Singapore Cinema?" in Mette Hjort & Duncan J. Petrie (Eds). *The Cinema of Small Nations.* Edinburgh: Edinburgh University Press.

Virilio, Paul. (2002). *Ground Zero.* (Chris Turner, Trans.). London: Verso.

von Sacher-Masoch, Leopold. (1999). *Venus in Furs.* (Jean McNeil, Trans.). New York: Zone Books.

Zielinski, Siegfried. (1999). *Audiovisions: Cinema and Television as Entr'actes in History.* Amsterdam: Amsterdam University Press.

Zizek, Slavoj. (1991). *Looking Awry: an Introduction to Jacques Lacan through Popular Culture.* Cambridge: The MIT Press.

_____. (2000). *The Ticklish Subject: The Absent Centre of Political Ontology.* London: Verso.

_____. (2002). *Welcome to the Desert of the Real.* London: Verso.

_____. (2003). *The Puppet and the Dwarf: The Perverse Core of Christianity.* Cambridge: The MIT Press.

_____. (2004). *Organs without Bodies: On Deleuze and Consequences.* London: Routledge.

I'm closer to the Golden Dawn
Immersed in Crowley's uniform
Of imagery
I'm living in a silent film
Portraying
Himmler's sacred realm
Of dream reality
I'm frightened by the total goal
Drawing to the ragged hole
And I ain't got the power anymore
No I ain't got the power anymore

I'm the twisted name
on Garbo's eyes
Living proof of
Churchill's lies
I'm destiny
I'm torn between the light and dark
Where others see their targets
Divine symmetry
Should I kiss the viper's fang
Or herald loud
the death of Man
I'm sinking in the quicksand
of my thought
And I ain't got the power anymore

Don't believe in yourself
Don't deceive with belief
Knowledge comes
with death's release

I'm not a prophet
or a stone age man
Just a mortal
with the potential of a superman
I'm living on
I'm tethered to the logic
of Homo Sapien
Can't take my eyes
from the great salvation
Of bullshit faith
If I don't explain what you ought to know
You can tell me all about it
On, the next Bardo
I'm sinking in the quicksand
of my thought
And I ain't got the power anymore

- David Bowie: *Quicksand*

Wissenschaftlicher Buchverlag bietet

kostenfreie

Publikation

von

wissenschaftlichen Arbeiten

Diplomarbeiten, Magisterarbeiten, Master und Bachelor Theses
sowie Dissertationen, Habilitationen und wissenschaftliche Monographien

Sie verfügen über eine wissenschaftliche Abschlußarbeit zu aktuellen oder zeitlosen
Fragestellungen, die hohen inhaltlichen und formalen Ansprüchen genügt,
und haben **Interesse an einer honorarvergüteten Publikation**?

Dann senden Sie bitte erste Informationen über Ihre Arbeit per Email
an info@vdm-verlag.de. Unser Außenlektorat meldet sich umgehend bei Ihnen.

VDM Verlag Dr. Müller Aktiengesellschaft & Co. KG
Dudweiler Landstraße 125a
D - 66123 Saarbrücken

www.vdm-verlag.de